The Revd Graeme Dav........ ....,...an priest in the UK, the USA and New Zealand. He is a religion and ethics columnist, a relationships counsellor and a lecturer in psychology. He is the editor of the *Theological Editions* website and has written several books, including *Anyone Can Pray* (SPCK, 2008).

WHEN THE VOW BREAKS

Contemplating Christian divorce

Graeme Davidson

An earlier version of this book was originally published in New Zealand
in 2005 as *Split Decision* by Zenith Publishing

First published in Great Britain in 2009

Society for Promoting Christian Knowledge
36 Causton Street
London SW1P 4ST

British Library Cataloguing-in-Publication Data
A catalogue record for this book is available from the British Library

ISBN 978-0-281-06153-2

1 3 5 7 9 10 8 6 4 2

Typeset by Graphicraft Limited, Hong Kong
Printed in Great Britain by Ashford Colour Press

Produced on paper from sustainable forests

*Thanks to my wife, Zena, for her loving support,
research assistance and editing talents*

Contents

Contents

Contents

Illustrations

Figures

Tables

Introduction

A friend from abroad, whom I met again after many years, told me her husband had developed serious psychiatric problems and, because of his erratic and self-destructive behaviour, she now spent much of her time caring for him. She then asked, 'Is it justifiable to cut the knot and seek happiness with someone else, or should I stay and continue to do my duty by my sick husband, as I promised on my wedding day?'

She had expected her marriage to last, but now wanted to discuss the ethical issues of when, if ever, it is right for a Christian to leave a committed relationship and whether her case qualified.

She questioned whether the kingdom of God and the good of families, spouses and others were ever served by those who insisted couples stay in marriages that had long ceased to function as God intended. But even if she felt imprisoned to a life of servitude by her marriage, would that give my friend the right to abandon her husband for the sake of her happiness? His future happiness and quality of life is also important. Although she came to realize she loved her husband too much to leave him, my friend's predicament raises many issues for which there are no simple answers.

From over 40 years' experience, first as a clinical psychologist and counsellor and then as an Anglican priest working in New Zealand, the UK and the USA, I found that no matter which partner instigated the split, most people were bewildered and upset when their relationship went wrong and they wished it were otherwise. Most tried their best to do the right thing, and my training as a theologian and priest, philosopher and ethicist was as important to helping their decision-making as my background in psychology and counselling.

It got me thinking of other situations where there are guidelines for breaking the rules. Issues of sanctity of life came to mind, especially when it is right to go to war. Like relationship break-ups, war creates havoc and extreme misery, sometimes lasting for generations. Yet most Christians accept that occasionally, as a last resort, war is a justifiable necessary evil. Although there remains much debate about the rules for a just war, the key principles are now incorporated in United Nations resolutions and international law, such as the Hague and Geneva Conventions.

In contrast, there have been different laws passed in different states and countries as to the grounds for divorce, but no clear set of principles and guidelines to help you decide whether your marriage is over and whether you should move on or stay in your relationship. This book provides Christian principles and guidelines that I believe meet this lack.

I experienced a divorce. I do not discuss this in depth elsewhere in this book as my experience is one of many and is typical of what often happens. However, it has made me aware in a very personal way of what is involved in a break-up. Robin, my wife of 26 years, dropped the bombshell over a cup of tea: 'I no longer feel we have much in common and I've decided to leave you.' There was no one else involved.

I loved Robin and thought we were happily married. I guess I was deluded. The pain of parting was like heart surgery without anaesthetic. I tried to do everything to save our marriage, which I mention in Chapter 7. But Robin had made up her mind. I respected her decision and felt I had unwittingly contributed to her unhappiness. I tried to understand why she felt as she did and to learn from the experience.

Like many couples, we parted amicably and shared in the upbringing of our then-teenage son. Seven years after the separation, I married Zena, who had prayerfully made the difficult decision to leave her husband after 18 years of marriage. They shared custody of their two children. Zena and I are happily married and our three, now adult, children enjoy one another's friendship and support. Sadly, Robin died of cancer a few years after our separation. We were all deeply affected by her death and it's hard to think of her not being there as a friend and mother.

I hope this book will help you understand how relationships can break down and what happens when you reach the decision zone. The Christian principles and guidelines provided are there to help you consider God's will for you and to make a prayerful, informed choice. This book may also help those who have already separated to better understand what happened, to affirm what was right, to avoid repeating mistakes in the future and to be assured of God's healing love.

1

On earth as in heaven

Ordained by God

Marriages are made in heaven, but we live on earth – with someone we've promised before God to have and to hold and be true to for better or worse, richer or poorer, in sickness and in health, until parted by death. If you marry young, that could be another 50, 60 or 70 years.

On our wedding day we believe we are marrying a lifelong friend and soulmate to share our innermost thoughts and feelings. We definitely expect a lifetime of intimacy and fun together, and probably children too. Even though it will be tough at times, we consider our love strong enough to forgive each other's failures and mistakes. And we probably believe that going through the dark valley of crisis, hardship and pain will strengthen our marriage so that, by the time we reach our fiftieth wedding anniversary, our marriage will be much stronger than it was on the fifth.

Couples who marry outside the Church and those who forsake marriage in favour of living together – now the majority of couples – would agree with these aspirations. Christian weddings, though, have another aspect: God is involved. We believe marriage is ordained by God. He approves of men and women fulfilling their God-given desires to unite in wedlock and 'become one flesh' (Gen. 2.24; Mark 10.6–9).

Even if Christians have a secular wedding, or one of the partners is non-Christian, we still regard their marriage as ordained by God. That doesn't mean God will work miracles to ensure the newlyweds live the rest of their lives in conjugal bliss, nor does it mean the

1

couple who prays together stays together. Far from it. In the UK, around 45 per cent of marriages end in divorce and Christian couples split at about the same proportion of the population as non-Christians.

Deciding whether to leave your spouse is rarely easy. When Christians divorce, we break our promises to each other and to God. The split seems to be a denial of what is at the very heart of the Christian gospel – God's reconciling and healing love. Yet, despite the seriousness of our wedding vows, are there circumstances where it is God's will that we forsake our partner? I believe that when a marriage can no longer function as God intended, the marriage is over.

Start-up failures

As a priest, I've had spouses return within a few months of their wedding telling me the relationship has failed and asking about annulment – how they can get the marriage declared invalid for legal or religious reasons. One bride even fled the nuptial bed while wedding guests were still celebrating the couple's union. Another man said 'I do' without letting his new wife know that he was not yet divorced from another woman.

Like many clergy, I had taken time to counsel these couples before the wedding to help them understand the nature of a Christian marriage and to encourage them to look at potential difficulties and ways of coping with them. In each case while I was counselling the couples, I thought they might not have enough in common, but I certainly didn't want to be paternalistic and tell them what I thought of their chances – it's likely they would have rejected my assessment anyway – and I could have been wrong. Nevertheless, I did my best to raise questions about the length of their friendship, what they thought of each other's friends and family, how they would react if they learned their partner had misled them or didn't want children, whether there were times when they felt embarrassed or didn't like what their intended said or did, and so on. But they were in love and wanted a church wedding in a sacred and picturesque setting, and to them that's what mattered most at that time.

The bride who leapt from the wedding bed rushed back to a lover her husband knew nothing about. She had pretended to her future husband that she was a virgin and was adamant they wait until the wedding night to be sexually intimate. It was only then that she realized her heart didn't belong to him and any intention to keep her marriage vows was a sham. On this basis their marriage was legally annulled, which means it was never a legal marriage.

The man who wasn't divorced from his first wife was found guilty of the crime of bigamy and this marriage was annulled too.

In both these cases the innocent spouse was devastated.

There are only a few hundred legal annulments granted each year in the UK. However, Church authorities may accept independently that a marriage is invalid for religious reasons. For Roman Catholics, in particular, this gives the go-ahead for remarriage in church after a civil divorce.

Others who came to me when their marriages ended in early separation were understandably upset and confused about what went wrong. Despite high hopes of success, these start-up marriages fail in the first few years in a similar way to many start-up commercial ventures.

None of the couples I had counselled before their short-term marriages had married cynically for immigration reasons, wealth, fame or other personal gain. Even the woman who had a secret lover wanted to start a new and better life with a good man whom she admired and respected. It took the wedding night for her to appreciate she really belonged with her lover.

These couples were in love, but at least one of the partners quickly realized their marriage was a mistake. One British survey even found that about a quarter of divorced women recalled having doubts about whether their marriage would last as they walked down the aisle. Should they have to live with that mistake for the rest of their lives? Should we continue to regard the engagement time as sufficient preparation? What about the majority of couples in the UK who cohabit for years before they marry: isn't that a good trial for a successful marriage? We'll be revisiting these questions when

3

we look at compatibility and how marriage breakdowns occur. We'll also consider whether these unions are salvageable.

If we survive the start-up problems, ahead is still the patch – after several years – when the honeymoon period is really over and dissatisfaction with our partners may peak. Most British divorces occur after six years of marriage, with the peak at around seven years – the so-called seven-year itch.

Let's look at four key examples of marriage breakdowns, which we will be referring to throughout the book.

Incompatibility

Harry had spent his young adulthood working hard to achieve academic success at the expense of his social life. A year into his first job as a lecturer in a prestigious university, he met a 16-year-old schoolgirl at an inter-church function and they fell in love. Everyone thought it was immature infatuation, with Emma treating Harry, who was 12 years older than her, as a father figure. So, when Emma left school to work in a factory and they announced their engagement, relatives and friends were concerned that the only thing they had in common was a strong physical attraction for each other. Ignoring their warnings, the couple married when Emma became pregnant. But the cracks soon appeared. Emma was easily bored and wanted to socialize with her teenage friends, while Harry expected her to be a homemaker and be supportive of him. They worked hard at making the marriage work, with each making compromises, and they went for marriage counselling and prayed for their relationship, as did their church friends.

The odds were stacked against them. Researchers find we have a higher chance of splitting if we have a low income, a pregnancy prior to marriage, wide differences in intellect or personality type, or different religious faiths. The risk increases if friends and relatives had their doubts about our relationship, if we've said 'I do' at a young age, if either partner has previously split from a marriage or similar relationship, if either partner has previously been promiscuous or either set of parents has split.

A number of these factors applied to Harry and Emma. Their relationship continued to worsen, until near their seventh anniversary, Emma announced,

> I was too young to know what I was doing when we married and I don't want us to spend the rest of our lives like we are. We've done all we can to make it work. You and I are different. We have our wonderful son but he's all we have in common. I think we should split. We can still be friends and good parents.

Neither Harry nor Emma had gone through the typical teenage and young adult apprenticeship in love where they'd learn about emotions and intimacy in relationships, equipping them to choose a lifelong partner. Was their incompatibility and inexperience in romance when they started out reasonable grounds for contemplating a divorce? After all, many partners rejoice in their diversity and regard their differences as strength rather than weakness.

Harry and Emma did stay together, but they lived increasingly separate lives, especially after their son started school. Like many married couples, their marriage was a functional but not very happy one. Would they, and their son, be better off if they separated and sought partners with whom they were more likely to be compatible? Or would this be like treating marriage as a disposable consumer product – to discard when it isn't working properly?

Infidelity

Kate found herself sharing her personal problems with Steve at an office party. He offered her a ride home and continued to listen attentively over coffee as she poured out her soul. A hug of empathy from Steve and a kiss of gratitude from Kate soon led to their making love. Afterwards, Steve felt so guilty that he told his wife and asked for her forgiveness.

Like most spouses who first learn their partner is unfaithful, Sue was devastated that Steve could betray her after years of trust and loyalty.

Steve accepted Sue's anguish as his just deserts. But his remorse turned to resentment after he'd spent several months condemned to sleep in the guestroom while she continued to sulk and treat him as a pariah. 'You're overreacting. It was only sex. It just happened. It didn't mean anything', Steve protested.

He reiterated that this was his only indiscretion and he didn't want any secrets between them: 'Most partners have affairs and most come through to have a stronger marriage. So why couldn't we do the same?'

Despite what Steve thought, adultery is not as common as the press and fictional dramas might lead us to believe. British and American research suggests that the vast majority of us disapprove of infidelity – even though about one-in-five husbands and about one-in-seven wives have sex with someone other than their partner at some point during their marriage. This is most likely to happen in the early years of the marriage and is often a one-night stand after a few drinks, as happened with Steve. Those who have longer-standing affairs usually do so with a mutual friend, and in most cases this happens when the marriage is already shaky, adding to the likelihood of a marriage split.

Adultery is legal grounds for divorce in the UK, and because it can hasten the process, it's the main reason given for British break-ups. It accounts for over a quarter of divorces, with more men than women being cited as unfaithful.

Affairs can be an exciting sexual adventure and an ego boost for those involved, but they usually happen through the need for someone who will understand and provide emotional support rather than for a better orgasm. Steve empathized with Kate and having sex with her was his way of reaching out to make her feel better. In fact, those who've had affairs often say the sex is better at home, and, because the feelings of conflict of loyalty are so difficult to deal with, they wish they'd never strayed. Some platonic and internet affairs can be just as heartbreaking and damaging to a marriage as sexual infidelity because the spouse's emotional focus is on someone else.

As Steve and Sue had been happily married for 17 years, should Steve have told Sue that he'd slept with Kate? She may have guessed anyway from the way Steve behaved when he got home, but many in this situation would lie about their infidelity to save their marriage. Even if your spouse believes in Christian principles of forgiveness, confessing that you've been unfaithful will test your relationship and increase your chances of a break-up. That raises the question of what an unfaithful Christian spouse should do. Lie to keep the marriage intact? Or tell the truth and risk disharmony and divorce?

What if you choose to lie and your deceit is discovered? Won't that make the betrayal worse? That's a difficult question, which we'll look at in more detail later. Steve is right in saying confession can lead to a stronger marriage, but only if both partners are willing to work on the relationship; and it may take several years to build trust again.

Sue was angry that, while Steve accepted the blame, he acted like he was the victim. As the standoff worsened, they both dredged up things they didn't like about each other. Dealing with Steve's pendulum swings between remorse and resentment and her own grief over his affair left Sue feeling increasingly miserable. She couldn't face the tension any longer and announced she was leaving him. 'Don't be so ridiculous and melodramatic', was Steve's response, which infuriated Sue and added to her determination to seek divorce on the grounds of adultery.

The consequences of the split following Steve's affair-and-tell were typical. Steve and Sue divided assets so that each had a lower standard of living. Steve also had to pay alimony and child support to Sue. Their two teenage children showed signs of emotional distress and their schoolwork suffered when they had to change school, make new friends and split their time between two homes.

Sue and Steve were so angry with each other that meetings about the children's welfare deteriorated into sniping sessions. Family members were upset but remained supportive of their own. Mutual friends tried to stay friends with both, sided with one or other of the partners or distanced themselves. Kate hinted to Steve that she was available if he was interested but he knew that if he became involved with her, it would confirm to Sue that she was right. Besides, he was still grieving too much over the end of his marriage to even think of another relationship for the meantime.

Incapacitated

Monica and Gerard had been married 22 years when Gerard became concerned over the way Monica was becoming easily stressed and forgot things, especially information she'd taken on board only moments before. Memory tests and a brain scan revealed she was suffering the early onset of the degenerative and fatal Alzheimer's disease. She was 46. Her care placed a major burden on Gerard and their three adult children, until Monica's memory loss, confusion, mood swings and lack of control over bodily functions became too big a problem. Gerard paid a trained carer to be with her while he was at work and continued to look after her in the evenings. That enabled the family to cope for another 18 months until Monica had to be hospitalized. She now reacted to Gerard's visits as if he was a stranger. Throughout her decline, Gerard grieved over what was happening to the woman he dearly loved and was powerless to cure, until he confided to me, 'Monica is now only a tiny thread of the rich tapestry she once was. As much as I love her, our marriage is in name only.'

Gerard started dating another woman and they were soon living together. His children were happy for their father and glad he was not relying on them quite so heavily for emotional support. Others in the community had mixed feelings.

Some agreed with the children: 'There's nothing wrong with him sleeping with someone else as his wife will never know and no one gets hurt.'

A few were disapproving: 'How could he take advantage of his wife's condition by bringing another woman into their home?'

Some thought Gerard should have divorced Monica first. But Gerard refused, arguing, 'I know I haven't been faithful, but I'm certain Monica would understand. I still love her and I promised to stay married to her for better or worse until parted by death. That's what I plan to do.' He continued to oversee her care and finances.

His new partner was supportive but she was keen to marry Gerard rather than continue living in an indefinite de facto arrangement dependent on Monica's lifespan; doctors advised it could be another eight years before she died. Gerard's partner commented: 'Married for life doesn't mean a life sentence when a marriage has effectively ended. If I were in a similar position to Monica, I would expect Gerard to remarry.'

Is this a case of Gerard being inconsistent in the way he keeps his wedding vows by saying that it's okay to commit adultery but not to divorce? Is he being fair on his new partner by sticking to the letter of his vow of lifelong commitment rather than the spirit? Or does a lifelong partnership mean life, no matter what the circumstances?

Emotional needs not met

Michael and Lisa had been married for 23 years and had a daughter at university. Lisa was feeling listless and neglected:

> Mike's a good man, but we don't seem to communicate like the great friends we once were. He's obsessed with his work, and when he comes home, he blobs out in front of the TV. Each of us is going our separate way and I feel bored, frustrated and unhappy. I've tried to talk to him and encourage intimacy but he avoids me except when he wants sex, which, thankfully, isn't often. And when we do, it's more about satisfying his urges than meeting my need for recognition and tenderness. He's oblivious of how I feel, which is stressful for me. He says I'm uptight and menopausal but he won't accept he's part of the problem. There doesn't seem much point in staying now our daughter is independent.

Although infidelity is the most common reason given to the courts for divorce in the UK, women are increasingly complaining of neglect, emotional insensitivity and lack of appreciation. They may express this as a communication problem, drifting apart or living on two different planets.

Many partners like Lisa won't tolerate staying in an unhappy relationship for long. Easier divorce processes, fairer divorce settlements and the widespread acceptance of divorce and single parenting have removed the stigma formerly associated with marriage break-up. The increasingly transient nature of our work and lifestyle weakens loyalties and reinforces the need to look after Number One. Our emphasis on consumerism contributes to the attitude that relationships are disposable. We no longer bow to the influence exerted by extended family and community, including the Church.

Michael was relatively content with the way things were. So he was stunned when Lisa said she was leaving. He knew that much of the excitement and romance had gone from their relationship but he thought that was all part of the natural process of growing old together. He couldn't understand why Lisa was adamant that they had grown apart and there didn't seem much point in her staying. An argument followed.

MICHAEL: We have our daughter and our history as a couple – all those wonderful times together. We'll be dividing what we own, so we'll both end up with a lower standard of living. And finding another partner . . . you end up exchanging one lot of problems for another. Why would you want to put both of us through that? And by leaving me, you're breaking your lifetime guarantee to stay until one of us dies. How do you feel about that?

LISA: Do you really think God wants us to stay miserable for the rest of our lives? You say you're happy, but I know you're not and I don't think God's a sadist. We had good times together and, yes, we do have a wonderful daughter. Now we're going to have a second chance. Isn't that what Christianity's about? I know I'll be happier on my own, even if I don't find someone else, but going our separate ways will give us both that chance.

MICHAEL: Because you've had a Road to Damascus experience, I have to suffer a divorce I don't want? Does what I think matter or are you only interested in what you want for yourself?

Is Lisa's response that God isn't a sadist who wants us to stay miserable in our marriages and that Christianity is about offering unhappy spouses a second chance an excuse? Or is it a serious theological consideration? Have Christians in the past put too much emphasis on sticking to the letter of the marriage vow, even if the marriage is loveless, rather than the principle of mutual love and happiness? Or is Michael right in identifying the quest for personal happiness in marriage as a hedonistic – rather than Christian – motivation?

Even if they believe there's little prospect of finding someone else, women who are unhappy in a marriage are usually prepared to make sacrifices to leave. About two times more women than men initiate leaving a marriage in the UK. Maybe this is because they are more in tune with the feeling aspect of relationships than men are. Many studies show that men tend to be happier in marriage than women and are less likely to consider divorce. Women tend to be more concerned than their husbands with the home, the emotional and intimate quality of the relationship and the welfare of the children. This makes them more likely to pull the plug on the marriage when these aspects are unsatisfactory. If Lisa does become involved with another man, there's a good chance that the two of them will live together rather than marry. If men instigate the leaving, they often do so because they are strongly attracted to another woman and intend to remarry.

Despite Michael's protests and both of them undergoing counselling, Lisa still left him. Michael found this difficult to accept and explained to others, 'This is a phase she's going through. I'm certain she'll come to her senses and realize what our marriage means.'

He tried to win Lisa back, which Lisa found annoying as she wanted to move on with her new life. But she also realized that, as she had sprung her decision on Michael, he would need time to grieve, beginning with denial and anger. Eventually, Michael recognized there was nothing he could do. He reluctantly agreed to a divorce after the statutory two-year period of separation. But he still felt strongly that Lisa's reasons for leaving were petty and selfish, while Lisa considered Michael would never understand her unhappiness. Had Lisa made the right decision for the right reasons, or could their relationship have been saved? As they were both members of a church congregation, would special prayers for Michael and Lisa's marriage or attending a Christian marriage enrichment group have helped them stay together?

Double jeopardy

Those of us who initiate leaving a marriage may feel a sense of relief once the stress of making the decision is over. Nevertheless, even though we may justify leaving to ourselves and maybe also to others, we can still feel upset at being the one who is breaking the wedding vow.

Our decision may cause deep pain to our partner, especially if, like Michael, he or she wasn't expecting a break-up. Both of us will probably feel sad that our marriage didn't survive and we'll feel we've let ourselves, and everyone we love, down. It's likely to raise doubts about our ability to make wise judgements about future relationships and it will take time to restore our confidence.

As Christians, we face a double jeopardy when we divorce. As well as feeling we've let ourselves and others down, we can also be acutely aware of letting God and the Church down because we weren't able to keep our sacred promise. Married clergy who divorce may feel it even more intensely, seeing their inability to achieve reconciliation as a negative witness to those to whom they minister.

Yet we Christians do reluctantly leave marriages, or find ourselves wondering why our partner left us and whether we weren't to blame. Some of us may even curse being Christian or vent our anger on God for not intervening and making our marriage a foretaste of heaven.

After the split, some of us may feel embarrassed by what has happened and change parishes or join a different denomination. Pentecostal groups, in particular, attract many divorcées seeking the emotional support of other Christians from broken relationships and the reassurance of God's healing love. However, some of us may feel so humiliated that we stop praying or attending church.

Until recently, the Church was not overly welcoming of the divorced. They were seen as sinners or flawed in some way, even if the divorced partner attending church had fought hard to save the marriage. For this reason, some Christians who split chose to remain separated rather than divorce. These days, the Church is less judgemental and more welcoming, but the stigma of breaking a holy vow is still felt by many, and the way the Church promotes family values can rub salt in the wounds of those whose families are broken.

St Paul reminds us how, 'all have sinned and fall short of the glory of God' (Rom. 3.23). Even if we feel shame at breaking the three-way vow between God, our spouse and us, should we regard ourselves as being like St Peter and the other disciples who broke their promise to stand by Jesus during his passion, or accept God's forgiveness and move on?

2

Love and marriage

Romance

We are weaned on fairy stories telling how, despite overwhelming obstacles and the interference of others, love conquers all and the prince and princess live happily ever after.

Some of us make jokes about frogs turning into toads instead of princes, and Cinderellas who become ugly sisters after the wedding. Yet, despite the scepticism, our romantic notions are so deep rooted they shape our own hopes and aspirations. And when we fall in love, the initial euphoria supports all those fairy tales of love conquering all and everyone living happily ever after. This is reinforced by our Christian belief that through God's love we can conquer all adversity (Rom. 8.28–38).

God's love can conquer adversity. That was what happened with Jesus' death and resurrection, which is a wonderful metaphor for how through the grace of God we can bury our old sinful life and begin anew through his redeeming love. It's a great promise of hope. But does it also imply that we can bury a dead marriage and start again without our spouse? We all make mistakes and the gospel message is about forgiveness rather than suffering the burdens of guilt and shame. And many of us do make mistakes in the partner we marry.

Compatibility

We idealize what we think we want in a mate – maybe someone attractive and interesting with a good income, intelligence, humour; someone who's sensitive and attentive, scintillating in conversation, and with a strong Christian faith.

14

Basically, though, we're genetically programmed to seek partners for their reproductive potential. That means someone who's physically attractive to us right down to how they smell and taste when we first kiss. This could explain why Harry married the much younger Emma, mentioned in Chapter 1, pp. 4–5. Maybe Emma unconsciously sought a man who could support her and father intelligent children, while Harry basically wanted a young, strong woman as a child-bearer and nurturer.

There's plenty of research to support this view, including speed-dating studies of single men and women. Speed daters attend a social event where they meet someone of the opposite gender for a few minutes – the speed date – then go on to meet others in the same way. Afterwards, they privately select the individuals they would like to know better. Despite what participants say is important in a mate, including their religion, previous marital status, intellect, personality type, or whether they smoke, researchers found most made their assessment within a few seconds, based largely on physical attraction.

Although opposites do attract and seem to complement each other's strengths and weaknesses, the difference in abilities and personality styles may soon lead to conflict, best summarized in the quip: opposites attract, then they attack.

A Cornell University study of 978 young heterosexual adults favoured the 'likes-attract' theory. According to research supervisor Stephen T. Emlen, 'humans use neither an "opposites-attract" nor a "reproductive-potentials-attract" decision rule in their choice of long-term partners, but rather a "likes-attract" rule'. We tend to look for the same things in a long-term partner as we see in ourselves. The researchers also found that good looks or money were not high on the list of what makes for a good mate. What came out on top were traditional family values.

Researchers using the popular Myers-Briggs® Type Indicator personality assessment find that the more personality type preferences couples have in common the more satisfied they are with their relationship. They also find the greatest problems come from extraverts who marry introverts, especially extraverted women who marry introverted men. Extraverts are energized by interaction with other people and focus on the external world. Introverts are the opposite. They focus on their internal world of ideas and concepts, and enjoy meditating or doing things on their own. The wife who needs to socialize and discuss her feelings can find it difficult to adapt to a husband who likes to keep his thoughts to himself. This may help explain why many unhappy wives complain of a communication gap and feeling lonely and unloved by their husbands, which is what happened with Harry and Emma.

Californian Christian marriage councillor and founder of the internet eHarmony dating service, Neil Clark Warren, claims 75 per cent of broken marriages are the result of couples who were originally mismatched. But nearly all of them didn't realize this when they married because they relied on the chemistry of love and physical attraction, which didn't last long. He maintains that despite the efforts of couples to make their marriages work, if they were originally mismatched the marriage usually fails.

Warren lists 29 dimensions, at least 25 of which we need to match – and maintain – for a relationship to succeed. At the top of the list are good character and quality of self-conception (knowing yourself). He explains that it's very difficult for a marriage to survive if one of you is not of good character and is prone to lie, cheat and steal for personal gain. It can also be difficult if one partner has emotional problems. Family background, intellect and spirituality come much higher on the list than sexual passion. Surprisingly, he places kindness, being able to adapt to each other and conflict resolution near the bottom.

Psychologist John Gottman came to a different conclusion over the importance of conflict resolution. He studied the reactions of hundreds of couples in his Family Research Laboratory in Seattle, checking heart rate, facial expression and how people talk about their relationship to each other and to other people. Of particular interest was the way they responded to conflict.

His finding seems obvious: a lasting marriage depends on a couple's ability to resolve conflicts. But he adds that not all conflict results in marital tension. He warns couples that their relationships are in trouble if they are marked by four characteristics, which he

16

calls the Four Horsemen of the Apocalypse – criticism, which can lead to contempt, followed by defensiveness and, finally, stonewalling or withdrawal. Gottman discovered that some of these factors were present before couples married and he maintains that this enabled him to predict with a high degree of accuracy which couples were likely to break up down the track.

He suggests seven principles that will help a marriage endure. These emphasize the importance of the couple making an effort to understand each other, create a positive supportive atmosphere where each partner is able to influence the other, work out effective conflict resolution methods, and find compromise and shared meaning that can avoid resentments.

If researchers like Warren and Gottman are right, the Church should be doing all it can through education and pre-marriage counselling to help couples who could be mismatched to recognize this. But, as I learned from the start-up marriages that I could see were unlikely to survive, couples in love are in no mood to discuss how they're unsuited. If we are ready to provide our prayers, support and help for married couples when their marriages start to come unstuck, we must be more willing to recognize also how people who marry in good faith often aren't suited for living a long married life together and need every chance to make amends and be able to start again.

Living together

As it can take many months for the euphoria and excitement of the initial love chemistry to wear off, it's wise to follow the traditional advice to take time to learn whether you and your loved one are compatible.

Does this mean you should spend time living together first?

Research has found that those who cohabit prior to marriage – especially women – tend to have unhappier marriages and, in the UK, they are three times more likely to divorce than those who don't live together beforehand. Maybe they started out when the chemistry was there but didn't have the heart to break up when it went. So they tried marriage to bring some magic back into their relationship.

Some studies have found couples who live together are less committed to each other and are not as happy as married couples. Statistically, their children don't perform as well at school, have more behavioural problems and are far more likely to suffer the consequences of their parents breaking up.

I think much depends on the couple's intention. For many in their late teens and early twenties, living together is often an experiment in sex and love, which typically lasts as long as the chemistry is there – less than a year. For others, it's merely a relationship of convenience, which they'll trade in for another. In fact, only about 5 per cent of UK couples who cohabit without intending to marry each other are still in relationships after 10 years.

Many who are older, especially those in their late twenties and early thirties who want to settle down with a partner, will move in together after they have spent time dating. They treat cohabitation as a time of betrothal where the intention is to stay together, which is what happens with about 60 per cent of British couples. Often, such couples will marry as a way of providing legal security when they have children.

The successful marriage

What is important in selecting a partner is spending time to learn about each other in different situations and social contexts, including with each other's family and friends. You should be at ease and enjoy being with each other as friends with no pretence, games or unrealistic expectations. You should also share a similar faith and have many of your values and interests in common.

No matter how wonderful the person you're dating is, or how much your family and friends like him or her, you have to know in your heart that the person is right for you. Be prepared to break up if you have a negative gut reaction or nagging feelings of unease. That may be hard to do as you don't want to cause pain, least of all to yourself.

As Christians, we believe that through perseverance and suffering, with the grace of God and the love of Christ working through us, we can effect changes in people. That is true, but we need to be careful not to romanticize Christianity and what we think God wants us to accomplish. God is unlikely to call us to marry someone to change them. As we shall learn in Chapter 4, God ordains marriage so we can have a partner who will be a companion and a helpmate, not a cause.

Interestingly, there is more research into what can go wrong with relationships than what makes for a successful long-lasting union. However, various studies of successful marriages have found some basic ingredients. The partners believe they are right for each other and that their marriage is sacred and binding. Their trust, understanding and high respect for each other remain constant through good times and bad. So do intimacy, affection, fun, humour, pleasure and emotional support, along with a mutually satisfying sex life. They agree on core aims, goals, values, religious beliefs and allow for conflict and differences. The couple are adaptable, have realistic expectations from the relationship and a willingness to live with each other's imperfections and personal idiosyncrasies. They also encourage each other's independence, but above all, they are the best of friends.

Stages in a marriage

Although there are wide variations in the way husbands and wives interact, most travel through several stages in developing their love relationship.

In the first romantic – or honeymoon – stage, which begins before we marry, we typically believe we have found Mr or Ms Right. We know we're in love and are loved. We feel happy and vibrant and see the world through rose-tinted glasses. We are passionate and would rather be in each other's arms than anywhere else. We easily overlook such idiosyncrasies as bad table manners, awful dress sense, our partner's habit of lateness or negative comments about our relatives. Although we don't have to climb glass mountains, slay dragons or spin straw into gold as the romantic heroes and heroines are expected to do in fairy stories, we are demonstrable in declaring our undying love. We defend our beloved against criticism and run up high telephone bills when we're apart. We send hundreds of emails and text messages to each other, make a fuss of birthdays and minor anniversaries and think nothing of sitting for ages in rush-hour traffic to meet our beloved. Men who scoffed at the thought of poetry will produce verse and women who spurned fashion will want to look glamorous to please their partner.

The relationship is easy at this stage. Differences in values, attitudes and upbringing seem as insignificant as the feud between the Capulet and Montague families did for Romeo and Juliet. Despite what others might think or say about us as a couple, we feel we belong together like daffodils and spring. We willingly expose innermost thoughts and feelings to each other, knowing we are accepted and loved for who we are. Any conflicts between us are endearing spats and it's fun to make up afterwards. Love is blind and we believe it conquers all.

This stage is important as it confirms how we can enjoy, nurture, support and satisfy each other as a couple without relying on others.

Then comes the hangover – or discontent – stage when the heartache can turn to headache. During this second phase of the relationship, those who have been totally smitten and head over heels in love are usually those who suffer the most disillusionment. Their Mr or Ms Right is now Mr or Ms Wrong.

At this stage there is nostalgia for what used to be. Partners may gaze at courtship emails and photos and wonder what went wrong. Counsellors often hear laments like: 'He used to buy me flowers and send me poems by email'; 'She used to wear sexy clothing and seduce me. Now she has to finish what she's reading or complains of being too tired.' While making love, partners think about shopping, who's going to win the next game, or imagine they're with someone else. It would take a life or death emergency before one of them would think of crossing town in rush-hour traffic to be with the other.

You have now awoken to the mundane reality of someone who doesn't always do things the way you want them done and who has unreasonable expectations of you. The polite requests that were once the command you gladly fulfilled are now a nagging nuisance. You're upset over derogatory remarks about your family, and are now embarrassed by your partner's table manners and the offbeat clothes. You, in turn, feel totally exposed to your partner's critical scrutiny.

There's a strong desire to reassert yourself as your own person. You might stay late at work, go out alone or with friends, or spend a large amount of money without consulting your partner. You're defensive about your rights and feelings. This can develop into power plays, competitiveness and acrimonious arguments that seem difficult to resolve. Accusations surface of unreasonableness, insensitivity, selfishness, nagging, stubbornness and neglect or lack of Christian virtues. You try to salvage the romance by replicating past romantic episodes and associations. But the enchantment has gone.

Partners may belittle each other and make snide comments to others. There's blame and faultfinding, such as: 'He expects me to run around after him', or 'She expects me to treat her like a spoilt princess.' Self-blame is often involved: 'I think I've made a terrible mistake. I was on the rebound?' 'I was infatuated and blinded by passion.'

It's common to confide in friends or turn to someone who is sympathetic, such as a former date or friend of your spouse. This could aggravate the situation through creating mistrust. It's not unknown to end in an affair with the sympathetic person, your affections temporarily transferred to him or her, which may explain in part why people who have been married only a short time score so high in infidelity statistics. Once such an affair happens, it can be very difficult to retrieve the relationship. Your partner, who's also in a state of discontent, will view it as proof of relationship breakdown.

For the relationship to survive the discontent stage, the couple needs to move through to the third stage, the accommodation – or realism – stage. This is when partners adjust to realistic expectations. You now accept that love doesn't conquer all and a partner's life-long habits are not likely to change overnight, if ever. You learn to respond to each other as real people and set aside notions of fault and blame.

At this point, couples come to appreciate individual differences, strengths and weaknesses, as well as what they have in common, and to devise ways of accommodating this in their relationship.

21

The accommodation is a working contract or understanding, often implicit rather than stated, about who does what and when. By trial and error and a willingness to adapt, partners learn when it's unwise to criticize the other's fashion sense or to interrupt while the other is reading the newspaper.

It's important to understand how issues are resolved. This might simply be by transaction:

You'll try not to make negative comments about my family and I'll try not to wipe the plate with my finger. We'll each take half a day in the weekend for ourselves, and spend at least three evenings a week having a meal together. We may agree to disagree on many things that we know we'll never resolve, but we'll still treat each other with respect.

Accommodation doesn't mean being false to yourself for the sake of another. Nor should it be dysfunctional co-dependency. That's where, to gain acceptance, one partner has to prove him or herself to the other. Thus, the dominant partner remains dominant by shifting the goalposts so that the other partner is always subservient and trying to please the dominant one. Unless there's true sharing, resentment and discontent will fester and surface in the future.

The fourth stage is the transformation – or maturity – phase. The couple appreciate the relationship is more than two individuals in a shared arrangement. They work to turn their union into something special and create support systems to make it happen. The couple might belong to an organization together and be supportive of each other's work and hobbies. Christian couples often mention how they feel bound by their mutual faith. This is the stage when couples feel they are great friends and enhance each other, but they also realize the relationship requires constant work, including making time for intimacy, romance, shared experiences and encouragement to develop as individuals.

Not all couples fit the template outlined in these stages. Those in arranged marriages may be motivated by a sense of duty rather than by romantic expectations. Others marry for reasons other than love and have established their own rules to co-exist. Then there are those

Love and marriage

who gradually grow in their love for each other without passing through the romantic phase – like those who marry the person next door or a colleague they have worked with for many years. There's a moment of revelation when they realize they belong together but, because they have known each other for so long, they have realistic expectations.

3

How marriages fail

Start-up discontent

Marriages fail in many ways, but they generally fall into one of three categories: start-up discontent, crisis discontent or creeping discontent.

Figure 3.1 is a simplified illustration of what can happen when the discontent descends after the romantic phase and triggers thoughts of leaving. Each negative incident after this – irritating habits, stressful and bitter conflicts, neglect, lack of respect, criticism and insults, unfulfilled emotional needs – adds to the original discontent so that the unhappy partner soon reaches the turning point where the decision is made whether to give the relationship another chance or to lament that it's all over and prepare to leave.

Start-up discontent also occurs when a partner has entered the relationship to satisfy an overriding selfish need. Typical reasons for these lopsided and obsessive relationships are: to escape a bad situation, for career advancement, to bolster self-esteem, to have a parent or former partner substitute, to resolve a sexual problem or addiction, to have a fairy tale wedding experience, desperation to avoid loneliness or to have a baby.

When the obsessive need is fulfilled or, alternatively, it's discovered that the relationship won't satisfy the need, the partner becomes superfluous. These one-dimensional relationships result in start-up discontent, taking one or both partners straight into the decision zone.

Crisis discontent

After the honeymoon, most of us learn to adapt to our partner. What is good in the relationship offsets any discontent. In his book *The*

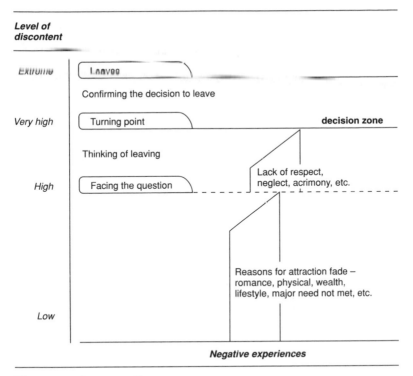

Figure 3.1 Start-up discontent

Seven Principles for Making a Marriage Work, John Gottman uses the analogy of an emotional bank account. Partners build up emotional savings through positive experiences together. There needs to be a high number of positive experiences to negative ones for the relationship to remain happy. Each partner can draw on this positive account when the relationship is under stress and conflict.

What happens, though, when a major crisis hits like the one-night stand Steve had with office colleague Kate, mentioned in Chapter 1, pp. 5–7, which ended Steve and Sue's marriage?

Figure 3.2 shows how a relationship can have typical incidents that cause differing levels of discontent, which couples accommodate. These fall within their expectations. There are enough positive experiences to offset these negative ones.

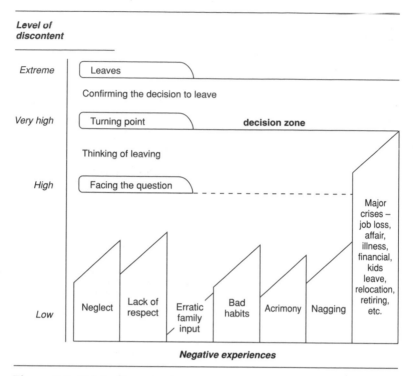

Figure 3.2 Crisis discontent

Then a crisis strikes and there aren't enough positives to offset this huge negative. The couple is unable to cope. This quickly pushes one or both partners into the decision zone.

Several crises may hit a relationship at once, like the death of a parent and then one partner losing a job because of serious illness soon after the couple have moved location. Couples may be able to cope with one or two crisis hits at a time but multiple strikes like this usually traumatize people and put huge strains on relationships.

Laid off from work after eight years of service, John sent his résumé to over 120 organizations and lost confidence when he didn't get a single interview. His wife, Ruth, was fully supportive and emphasized how, despite this setback, they still had their health and love for each other. They made budget cutbacks. But within a few months, John was drinking heavily, neglecting personal hygiene, sleeping erratically and watching television for long hours, while constantly venting his anger on Ruth. Their sex life deteriorated and soon ceased, which brought on more abuse.

John's employment crisis had brought them to the decision zone and Ruth prayed and raised the question with close friends and her parish priest whether she should leave him.

This story had a happy ending as John got a new job soon after. He told Ruth he was ashamed of his behaviour and thanked her for standing by him. But if he had remained unemployed for another six months, the outcome might have been quite different.

There are recognized phases in life when couples face more stress than at other times. Significant are the first months of pregnancy, especially unexpected pregnancy, and then when children are very young. Children reaching their teens may trigger a crisis by challenging their parents, and then by leaving home when their parents are in their late forties to middle fifties. This is when a wife may realize the husband she chose to be father to her children is not the person with whom she wants to spend the rest of her life. A husband may seek to recapture his youth or yearn for a younger woman to start another family.

With partners experiencing more financial independence, the number of people in their fifties who file for divorce in the UK has increased dramatically over recent years to make this the largest group of divorcees.

Creeping discontent

Many who reach the decision zone describe how the relationship has deteriorated over the years. Their complaints may seem trivial to others – like a partner spending too much time on his or her own interests or being constantly untidy. However, the errant partner mending his or her ways over these grievances seldom solves the problem.

Figure 3.3 shows how accumulated frustrations, dissatisfaction, resentment, boredom and hurt feelings mount. As the needs of one

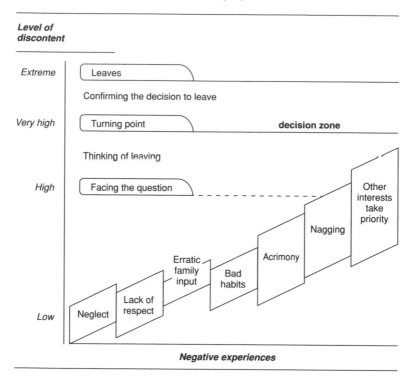

Figure 3.3 Creeping discontent

or both partners change, there can be insufficient adjustment to the changes. For instance, a spouse who has been home for the children when they are small may go back to work when they start school but continue to do the bulk of the housework.

Instead of acting as intimate partners who affirm each other, spouses then distance themselves from one another, living separate lives. Eventually, they reach a point where the creeping discontent becomes overwhelming. This brings the question of continuing in the relationship into the decision zone, which is what happened with Michael and Lisa, mentioned in Chapter 1, pp. 9–11. After 23 years of marriage, Lisa felt listless and neglected as she and Mike were no longer connecting with each other as they once did and her efforts to change the situation to her satisfaction had failed. Mike was relatively content with the way things were.

Facing the decision

Hollywood actor Mickey Rooney once quipped, 'Always get married in the morning. That way, if it doesn't work out, you haven't wasted a whole day.' The only break up I've known to happen that fast involved the bride who fled the nuptial bed for the arms of her lover, mentioned in Chapter 1, pp. 2–3. Around 80 per cent of us genuinely believe marriage is for life. Most people who have left a marriage still agree with this ideal and regret their marriage failure. It requires a major shift in our expectations before we seriously think of leaving.

If you're thinking of parting, you'll know you're very unhappy. But you'll also need to justify to yourself and God, as well as to your spouse, relatives and friends, why you want to break your sacred vow of till parted by death.

From his fieldwork and interviews with divorcing people, Joseph Hopper found we resolve the dilemma by rethinking our marriage. He suggests we begin by seeing our marriage in negative ways, often reaching back through our time together from when we were court-ing, to produce a history of problems. Maybe we think our partner had flaws or our personality differences meant we were incompatible. It dawns on us that our marriage is irrevocably flawed at its heart. It's a lemon – a false marriage that never really was a marriage and we shouldn't have promised our lives to each other in the first place.

Perhaps we kid ourselves that we were too naïve to understand what was involved or it could never work as we were from very different backgrounds. And, then, there's the diplomatic 'We love each other. But we were never meant to live together' – a perfectly good relation-ship ruined by marriage.

Naturally, if you're the spouse who doesn't want to leave, you'll react with anger or helplessness to any notion your marriage is a charade.

This pushes one, or possibly both, of you further towards the turning point and the decision to leave.

Figure 3.4 illustrates in detail what happens at the turning point. It shows how you move from discontent and thinking about leaving to considering it as a definite possibility. You might go through the decision zone phases quickly but you're more likely to progress slowly,

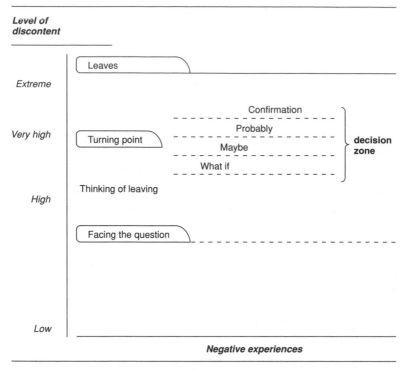

Figure 3.4 Detail of decision phases at the turning point

lingering for months or years at one place. You may even decide not to progress further and stay with your partner, as did Harry and Emma, mentioned in Chapter 1, pp. 4–5, despite their being incompatible through age, background and interests.

The first stage is the phase I've called the 'what if' phase, the second the 'maybe' phase, the third is the 'probably' phase, and the last stage the 'confirmation' phase.

'What if' phase

If you find yourself asking, 'What if I'd married someone else? What if I leave?' you'll be tossing up some big pros and cons and wondering how to decide between them.

You'll probably feel guilty about thinking of leaving and experience anxiety about the future. Trying to look at the question objectively, you may distance yourself from your partner. Then, seeing the impact you're having on the relationship and your partner, you may waver some more and want to alleviate his or her distress. This can send a false signal of reconciliation or of blowing hot and cold, which may confuse and anger your partner. If he or she asks what's wrong, you may be reluctant to tell the truth until you've finally decided.

Sometimes your partner may do something that will throw your ideas about leaving into disarray. It may be an unexpected romantic holiday, a night out together or spending quality time listening to your concerns. Some spouses do put up with a mainly negative relationship for these few treats. For most of us though, one or two good experiences are not enough to move us out of the decision zone.

Your marriage is salvageable at this point, if you and your partner are prepared to work on it.

'Maybe' phase

The 'maybe' phase is when you or your partner decides that there could be grounds for leaving. Imagining what it's like outside your marriage now becomes a question of whether it's a realistic idea. This is when your list of pros and cons is refined and weighted as evidence in favour of leaving.

A key piece of information might be enough to tip the balance. One woman told me how she envied her divorced friend's freedom to travel, go to the gym and take art classes – and to have romantic trysts with interesting men. It seemed so much more exciting than her own dull married life that she had replaced imagining 'what if' with thinking 'maybe I should leave'. When I next met her, I found she was using the 'maybe' phase to gain a more realistic picture of her friend's life. She realized her friend told her only the exciting bits and most of the time she went home after work to a soulless apartment and a lonely life, much like Angie in Chapter 5, pp. 60–1. Her friend's husband had remarried a younger woman and was having a second family. The woman began to question if she really wanted that to happen to her.

She instinctively pulled back from a lifestyle that she thought was going to be worse than her present situation and made a conscious decision to enjoy what was good with her husband. He, in turn, noticed the change in her attitude and became more responsive, and their relationship slowly improved.

So, it's still possible to save your marriage. But, if at this stage you don't pull back from thinking of separating, your arguments for leaving begin to firm up and it becomes harder to accept contrary views. Tentative plans for how you might go about leaving start to take shape and you distance yourself further from your partner to prepare for the break.

'Probably' phase

Partners who are at the 'probably' phase have gone past the turning point. They are in the process of confirming how the benefits of leaving outweigh those of staying.

You're now convinced your marriage wasn't made in heaven and God probably didn't intend you for each other after all. You're well into the process of emotionally distancing yourself from your partner. If he or she makes any attempts at reconciliation, you're likely to view them as too little too late, as insincere or pathetic.

You look even closer at what's involved with leaving and weigh the risks against future happiness. As well as talking to others who have been through a relationship break-up, you may take advantage of the internet and books to find answers.

You'll also begin to grieve over the loss of the relationship – even before the split has occurred. This includes mourning the loss of love and all the hopes and dreams you had for your relationship, as well as feeling anger and blame for its failure. You may feel depressed, weep and want to withdraw from others. Or you might direct your anger at your spouse.

It's very difficult to save the marriage at this point, even with counselling. Some couples take second honeymoons, go on holiday or do something special together. They may even reaffirm their wedding vows in church, but any positive effects are usually temporary or have the opposite effect. Many couples break up after a holiday because the intensity of the closeness magnifies the issues dividing them. Their desperate effort to save the marriage becomes, in effect, a symbolic farewell.

Confirmation phase

In the confirmation phase, you're still grieving but the chances of break-up move from probable to inevitable. You're now sure your marriage was a mistake, but you won't actually leave until you're a hundred per cent certain. Yet again, you'll examine reasons and adjust your thinking to going solo. You'll also decide how best to exit the relationship and make concrete plans for the future.

The marital disharmony, unhappiness and anxiety that led to your decision are now in the past. Although there's still the break-up and going solo to cope with, you know where you stand.

Relationship therapists and counsellors commonly see couples for the first time during this confirmation phase. One of the partners may be hoping for reconciliation. The other is treating it as a gesture, looking to the counselling as further confirmation of his or her decision to leave and something that will help them split amicably (exit counselling). It's possible that once you've decided to give up on the marriage, you'll unconsciously push your spouse into doing the actual leaving so that you can act the 'injured' party and assume the moral high ground. Examples of such sabotaging behaviour are withholding financial support, seeking incompatible activities or career options, withdrawal of intimacy and communication, making constant unreasonable demands, or your own infidelity (see Chapter 10, 'Leaving', p. 132).

Marriage indicator

Table 3.1 is a simple non-scientific check for symptoms of serious discontent.

Try to answer all the questions as honestly as you can.

Scoring and evaluation

The scoring is simple. Add the scores for all the answers. The result will be a score between 0 and 100.

It's presumptuous to try to draw a random line and say that if you get a score above where the line is drawn, then your marriage is great, and if it's below, it's in serious trouble. That's because the answer to

Table 3.1 Relationship self-check

Circle the answer that best describes the relationship between you and your partner.
4 = Nearly always; 3 = Often; 2 = Sometimes; 1 = Occasionally;
0 = Practically never

1 I trust my partner.	4	3	2	1	0
2 My partner is supportive of my career and objectives in life.	4	3	2	1	0
3 I feel safe around my partner.	4	3	2	1	0
4 I'm 'turned on' by the thought of sex with my partner.	4	3	2	1	0
5 We have similar religious convictions.	4	3	2	1	0
6 I can describe the important issues my partner faces.	4	3	2	1	0
7 I support my partner's main ambitions and goals in life.	4	3	2	1	0
8 We work together cooperatively as a team.	4	3	2	1	0
9 My partner treats me fairly.	4	3	2	1	0
10 We laugh and joke a lot when we are together.	4	3	2	1	0
11 We agree about money.	4	3	2	1	0
12 We agree about children and their upbringing.	4	3	2	1	0
13 We may not solve every issue, but we have ways of handling disputes that leave me feeling good.	4	3	2	1	0
14 My partner is good at listening to me.	4	3	2	1	0
15 I enjoy my partner's company and don't find him or her boring or irritating.	4	3	2	1	0
16 Our relationship allows me to be independent and to do what's important to me.	4	3	2	1	0
17 I look forward to spending time together.	4	3	2	1	0
18 I respect my partner.	4	3	2	1	0
19 My partner's personality and individual style is ·acceptable to me.	4	3	2	1	0
20 Our relationship satisfies me emotionally.	4	3	2	1	0
21 My partner values me and shows me consideration.	4	3	2	1	0
22 I know many of my partner's relatives and friends and get on well with them.	4	3	2	1	0
23 My relationship with my partner is a strong and binding one.	4	3	2	1	0
24 We both have similar political or other non-religious ideological convictions that are important to us.	4	3	2	1	0
25 Both of us make an effort to spend some special quality time together.	4	3	2	1	0

Score for each column

Add together column scores for total =   Maximum = 100

Table 3.2 Relationship self-check scores

85–100	Those who said they were very happy in their marriages got a score in this range. Usually both partners got a similar high score.
65–85	These partners admitted to problems and times of unhappiness in their relationship. Sometimes there was a difference in scoring between one partner and the other.
0–64	These partners had recently broken up or were about to. There was often a difference in scoring between one partner and the other. The partner who wanted the break-up, or who'd already left, usually scored below 45.

one question may be vital to the survival of the marriage. If you answered 'Practically never' to 'I trust my partner', that would tend to undermine the very basis of your relationship. Or if you put a circle around 'Practically never' for 'I feel safe around my partner', you could be in danger of serious harm.

Usually, though, symptoms come in clusters. You're more likely to get a high score if the relationship is very good and a low score if the relationship is doing poorly. In trials with many couples, I found that people fell roughly into the groupings shown in Table 3.2.

Remember, these results are indicative only and the intention is to provoke thought. It may be worth suggesting to your partner that he or she try the test so that you can compare and discuss the results. This could be a good way of affirming what's good in your relationship and looking at what needs to be improved. It may also help you realize you need to think seriously about whether to stay or leave.

4

Christians and divorce

Different views

Most Christians deciding whether or not to leave a partner look to the Bible and their church for advice. But that raises questions of which biblical passages and doctrines to focus on, how to understand them and which views are valid.

Do you concentrate on the words of Jesus in Matthew's Gospel, where he allows divorce only for adultery (Matt. 5.32; 19.9)? Or do you take more notice of his advice in Mark's Gospel, where he makes no exception and says that those who divorce and remarry sin by committing adultery (Mark 10.11–12)?

When Jesus reiterates from the Genesis creation account how couples are one flesh and what God joins no one is to separate, does that mean you're to stick with your partner no matter what? Or can you separate but not divorce and remarry?

Jesus tells us to leave a wife and family for the sake of the kingdom of God (Luke 18.29–30). Does this mean we can leave a spouse if we believe it's God's will? Is neglect a ground for divorce as it was for Hebrew slaves (Exod. 21.10–11)? Or, if the intimacy, affection and respect for each other has gone so that you feel lonely and like strangers to each other and attempts to rekindle the relationship have failed, does that mean your marriage is no longer serving its primary purpose of companionship as described in Genesis (Gen. 2.18)? Can that be grounds for divorce?

Jesus certainly criticized religious leaders of his time for being overly legalistic. Do some churches make the same mistake in their attitude to divorce and remarriage by refusing to recognize how love, forgiveness and having another chance are at the heart of the gospel?

Marriage and divorce in the Old Testament

Imagine you're a woman living in Israel in Old Testament times. According to the Hebrew Scriptures, your status as one of God's people is similar to that of a woman under the Taliban in Afghanistan today. But the rules governing your daily behaviour come from the Torah, or the law of the Covenant God made with Moses, and you learn them from your family and your religious leaders. You obey them because they are God's commandments. You fear punishment for sullying your family's good reputation, especially the honour of your menfolk. More than anything, you fear damaging your family's and the nation's relationship with God. You reflect these values in your demeanour and in how you intend to bring up your children.

While single, you're one of your father's assets and under his authority. Once you reach puberty, he will take great pains to protect you from any man who might want to seduce or rape you before he finds you a suitable husband to whose authority he transfers you at marriage. As most women are married in their early teens soon after puberty, your chances of straying are small.

Sexual activity with a man before you're married not only brings dishonour to your family but also greatly reduces your chances of marrying anyone else. You're second-hand goods, and you're damaged goods if you're pregnant or there could be doubt over the paternity of a firstborn child. This is about preserving the husband's bloodline and precisely why a messenger of God needed to persuade Joseph to marry Mary. As a betrothed couple, they were required to forego sexual relations until marriage but she was scandalously pregnant with Jesus, a child that wasn't Joseph's (Matt. 1.18–25).

If your family passes you off to a prospective husband as a virgin when you aren't, and he finds out after the nuptials, then your chances of actually staying alive beyond your wedding night are low. Your new husband will be looking for blood on the sheets from a broken hymen after first intercourse, and, if he can't find evidence of this, then it's up to your family to prove you were a virgin. If they can't, then you suffer the same fate as an adulteress – to be stoned to death (Deut. 22.13–21). In contrast, there's no mention of men having to abstain from sex with single women.

The prophets Hosea, Isaiah and Jeremiah all refer to the affection, love and devotion of a husband, but it's a man's world where most women have inferior status, are treated like chattels with a price and whose destiny is controlled by men.

Your marriage is a private contract between the head of your household and the head of your intended husband's household, similar to a property deal. While the dowry paid by your father remains your property, ensuring your welfare as long as you remain a faithful wife, if you commit adultery, you violate your husband's rights and forfeit the dowry – and possibly your life. Your lover, who defrauds your husband by taking you without permission or payment, also comes under the Deuteronomy 22 penalty of stoning to death.

The warnings against straying from the wedding bed in Proverbs (Prov. 5) would suggest that some were tempted despite the dire consequences if caught.

As your marriage is a legal contract rather than a sacred event, is it ordained by God?

Yes. In the first creation story in the book of Genesis, God creates men and women so they can have children.

> So God created man in his own image, in the image of God he created him; male and female he created them. God blessed them and said to them, 'Be fruitful and increase in number; fill the earth and subdue it.'   (Gen. 1.27–28)

If you bear plenty of children, especially sons, God blesses you, but if you're infertile, have miscarriages, stillborn babies or children who die as infants, then God has cursed you.

In the second creation story, God provided woman as a 'helper' so that 'a man will leave his father and mother and be united to his wife, and they will become one flesh' (Gen. 2.18–24). As a wife, you're there to assist your husband and, as part of his flesh, you join with your husband as the warp and weft combine to form cloth. In both accounts, marriage was part of God's created order. In other words, he ordained it.

Being one flesh implies monogamy – for a wife, but not necessarily for a husband. If your husband strays, he won't be dishonouring you. In fact, if you live before the Exile in Babylon during the sixth century BC and your husband is wealthy or of noble rank, then he may want to take other wives or concubines.

Unlike some other Middle East codes of the times, the Old Testament provides scant information on divorce.

Adultery, which is a common cause of divorce in the UK today, is contrary to the seventh and probably the best known of the Ten Commandments: 'You shall not commit adultery' (Exod. 20.14; Deut. 5.18). The fact that the religious authorities brought a woman caught in the act of adultery to Jesus to ask whether they should stone her to death as commanded in the law of Moses (John 8.3–11), suggests that there was debate during Jesus' time regarding adultery and the death sentence. It also raises the question of how rigidly the law regarding relationships between men and women was upheld in practice.

If there were any lawful grounds for divorce, they are not given. Nor do we have any indication how common divorce was. Deuteronomy says a man can divorce a wife who displeases him 'because he finds something indecent about her' (Deut. 24.1). The word 'indecent' in Hebrew literally means 'nakedness of a thing', which implies immoral behaviour, but what kind of immoral behaviour is unclear.

Several of the Old Testament prophets, especially Hosea, use an adulterous wife as a metaphor of how Israel is unfaithful to God. Jeremiah presents God himself as a divorcé, having sent Israel away with a certificate of divorce (Jer. 3.8).

During their exile in Babylon, many Jewish men married Babylonian women who worshipped their own gods. After the 50 years in Exile ended in 539 BC, these men where forced to divorce their wives and abandon them and their children before returning to the Holy Land. Intermarriage with people of other cultures and religions was an act of unfaithfulness to God (Ezra 10; Neh. 13.23–30).

As an Old Testament wife, you can't divorce your husband. Even if he has falsely accused you of sleeping with someone else before you were married, you can only initiate a divorce by appealing to the rabbinic court. Your husband has to enact it. He will probably say the divorce formula: 'she is not my wife, and I am not her husband' (Hos. 2.2) and then issue a divorce certificate in writing (Deut. 24.1). You're then both free to marry again. But you can't remarry your first husband if your second husband dies or divorces you (Deut. 24.1–4). Nor can you marry a priest (Lev. 21.7).

In his book *Divorce and Remarriage in the Bible: The Social and Literary Context*, David Instone-Brewer maintains that by the time of Jesus and the early Church, Jewish rabbinical thought was of the general opinion that divorce was undesirable but sometimes necessary for reasons of childlessness, material or emotional neglect and infidelity. Remarriage was generally accepted.

Marriage and divorce in the New Testament

Let's now imagine you're a Gentile wife with a non-Christian husband living in AD 165 under the Roman Empire on the Aegean Coast of Asia Minor, which we now call Turkey. Under Roman Law, divorce and remarriage is relatively easy and both men and women could initiate divorce, but the infant Church in Ephesus, to which you belong, has different standards.

Although the Old Testament understanding that you are your husband's property no longer applies to either Jews or Gentiles, you're still obliged to obey your husband as head of the household, analogous to the way Christ is the head and saviour of the Church, his body. And, as Christ loved the Church and gave himself for it, husbands ought to love their wives as their own bodies (Eph. 5.22–33; see also Col. 3.18–19).

As part of your Christian initiation, you learn how Jesus referred to the Book of Genesis and taught that marriage is more than a contract between two families. God joins the couple and marriage is permanent and inviolate: 'Therefore what God has joined together, let man not separate' (Mark 10.9). A spouse who divorces and remarries commits adultery, and this also applies to Gentile wives using Roman Law to divorce their husbands (Mark 10.12). Your church elders teach that Jesus emphasized love, forgiveness and faithfulness, so that even lusting after a woman is to commit adultery in the heart (Matt. 5.27–30). Although there's no mention of women lusting after men, you appreciate that this means Christians should do all they can to remain faithful and not be tempted or tempt others.

If your church has access to what we now call the New Testament writings, you'll know that Matthew's Gospel gives an exception for wives cheating on their husbands. During the Sermon on the Mount, Jesus says that whoever divorces his wife, 'except for marital unfaithfulness' (Matt. 5.32), causes her and any subsequent husband to become adulterers. If your teachers are Gentile Christians, they may not be aware that Jesus is referring here to the Hebrew practice of husbands lawfully divorcing their wives, never vice versa.

Later in Matthew's Gospel (Matt. 19.3), intellectuals from a religious faction known as the Pharisees ask Jesus, 'Is it lawful for a man to divorce his wife for any and every reason?'

Your teachers may not understand that the Pharisees were quizzing Jesus on which of their two factions was right, the Hillel, who permitted a man to divorce his wife on the pretext of virtually any fault he could find in her, or the Shammai, who allowed divorce only for adultery. As noted earlier, if an adulterer was stoned to death in accordance with the law (Deut. 22.22–27), then the Shammai position would be an academic one. The husband would be free to marry again anyway. But it appears the death penalty was rarely given in Jesus' day.

When Jesus tells them, 'what God has joined together, let man not separate' (Matt. 19.6), the Pharisees are confused and follow through with the obvious question: 'Why then', they asked, 'did Moses command that a man give his wife a certificate of divorce and send her away?' (Matt. 19.7).

Jesus responds by stating that Moses allowed them to divorce because they had hard hearts and that it wasn't originally like that. He then says that anyone who divorces his wife and remarries commits adultery, except, he repeats, for 'marital unfaithfulness'. The Greek word translated as unfaithfulness is *porneia*, which is not the usual word for adultery in the New Testament. Often translated as fornication, it has different meanings in different contexts. In this context, it would include any form of marital sexual misconduct on the part of the wife.

Jesus' answer seems straightforward enough, yet it disturbs the disciples listening to the debate. They comment that if it's going to be like that between husband and wife, then 'it is better not to marry' (Matt. 19.10). Is this because Jesus is demanding tough standards for marriage and they want the Hillel option of an easy divorce for husbands? Or could Jesus have also been using *porneia* as a metaphor for unfaithfulness to God?

Jesus answers the disciples by telling them that some can't marry because they were either born eunuchs or made that way by others, while others choose to renounce marriage for the kingdom of heaven. In other words, Jesus, like St Paul to come, seems to be suggesting that marriage can distract couples from focusing on the kingdom of God.

As a Gentile Christian, you would probably find some of Jesus' and St Paul's views on marriage confusing. Even though Jesus went to a wedding feast in Cana (John 2.1–11), you'd think he had a low opinion of married couples as he uses examples of marriage coming between people and God and how in the kingdom of God things are different (see Matt. 24.37–39; Luke 14.15–23; 20.27–39; Matt. 22.23–33; Mark 12.18–27).

Jesus tells his listeners that if they are to be his disciples they need to be prepared to hate their family, including their wife (Luke 14.26), and later he tells them to leave a wife and family for the sake of the kingdom of God (Luke 18.29–30). Despite what Jesus says about not divorcing, he now says we must put his kingdom ahead of wealth, family ties or anything else that might come between God and us.

If your non-believing husband opposes your faith as a Gentile Christian, does that mean you can divorce him to marry a devout Christian so the two of you can work together for the greater good of God's kingdom? As the kingdom comes first in Jesus' teachings, then leaving a spouse if you've good reason to believe it is God's will, does seem a possibility. However, if you suggested this to your church elders, it's unlikely they would concur.

You would also learn how St Paul reinforces Jesus' view of marriage as a lesser, imperfect state as it diverts spouses into concentrating on the worldly things of domestic life rather than what is of God. In his lengthy discussion on marriage to the fledgling Church at Corinth (1 Cor. 7), Paul wishes all men, widows and unmarried people were like him, presumably a chaste bachelor. He wants those who have wives to 'live as if they had none' (1 Cor. 7.29); he tells unmarried women, like a cynical agony aunt columnist today, that he wants to spare them the hassles of married life.

With advice like that, you may feel you've joined a weird ascetic sect which frowns on couples and wants those unfortunates who are married to avoid sex and stick to a spiritual relationship.

But having said that it is good if men don't marry and those who are married should avoid sex with their wives, Paul does concede marriage is necessary for those who 'cannot control themselves'. His is the famous saying: 'It is better to marry than to burn with passion' (1 Cor. 7.9).

'Do not deprive each other except by mutual consent and for a time, so that you may devote yourselves to prayer. Then come together again so that Satan will not tempt you because of your lack of self-control' (1 Cor. 7.5). What if one spouse wants to have sex and the other doesn't? The answer: wives are to submit to their husbands (Col. 3.18–19), but because they are one flesh husbands are to love and not abuse their wives.

Can you leave your husband if he abuses you or you fear for your life? Not according to Paul, who quotes 'the Lord': 'A wife must not separate from her husband. But if she does, she must remain unmarried or else be reconciled to her husband. And a husband must not divorce his wife' (1 Cor. 7.10–11). So, as you're married to a non-believer, you must stay with him because you sanctify him through being one flesh with him. Through your witness, according to Paul, you may even save him.

But Paul also states that if a Christian is married to an unbeliever and 'the unbeliever leaves, let him do so. A believing man or woman is not bound in such circumstances' (1 Cor. 7.15).

43

As the Hebrew Scriptures say God wants men and women to marry and have children and marriage was the norm for first-century Jews, why would Paul hope that early Christians would follow his chaste example? The reason Paul gives is 'time is short'. He was expecting Jesus' return during his own lifetime. So it's logical he was urging them to concentrate on preparing for this great event rather than getting distracted by such mundane matters as pleasing a spouse.

But you're a Gentile Christian wife 130 years later, and Jesus hasn't returned. His advent is still a glorious hope but Paul's advice about not marrying or about exercising self-control and abstinence in your marriage isn't quite so valid for you. Could it be time for your church to move closer in line with the culture you live in? Might it even be God's will that you leave your marriage for the glory of God?

Church teachings on divorce and remarriage

The Gentile church to which you belong would have been largely unaware of the Jewish context in which Jesus made his comments about divorce and remarriage and his use of the Aramaic language, whereas Jewish Christians would know the demands of the Torah, which says God ordained marriage primarily for a companion and a helper (Gen. 2.18), and the law of Moses denouncing marital neglect (Exod. 21.10–11).

The early Church also gave little importance to what Jesus said about leaving a wife and family for God's kingdom. Instead, they focused almost exclusively on Jesus' comments about not divorcing, except for infidelity, and how those who remarried broke the Seventh Commandment by committing adultery. Even the innocent party couldn't remarry while an ex was still alive. Some of the early theologians were harsher on divorce and remarriage than Jesus, while others raised the question of whether adultery should be the only exception.

One of the most popular and influential early Christian books your church elders would refer to would be the mixture of allegory, parables and teachings called *The Shepherd of Hermas* – also known as *The Pastor of Hermas* – written about AD 125. Hermas, a freed slave, describes his vision of a God-sent shepherd who advises a husband to give up a wife who persists in committing adultery. If the husband continues to stay with her out of loyalty when he knows she is committing adultery, that makes him complicit in her sin. If his wife won't repent, then he should divorce her and remain single. Hermas reiterates Jesus' teaching that if the husband remarries, he commits adultery. But he also gives a very Christian reason why the husband should remain single. It's to allow for the possibility of his wife repenting. 'Assuredly. If the husband do not take her back, he sins, and brings a great sin upon himself; for he ought to take back the sinner who has repented' (*The Pastor of Hermas* II.4.1).

The prolific early Christian writer, Tertullian (*c.* 160–*c.* 220) accepted divorce and remarriage, provided it happened prior to becoming a Christian. Once a person became a Christian, then his or her marriage was indissoluble, even after death. He claimed that if a woman remarried after her husband's death, 'This will be adultery, the conscious affection of one woman for two men' (*Treatises on Marriage and Remarriage* Part Fourth; *On Monogamy* X).

An influential third-century theologian, Origen (*c.* 185–*c.* 254), noted in his *Commentary on Matthew* how some church leaders had allowed divorced women to remarry while their husbands were still alive. As well as adultery, Origen asks whether other monstrous acts would be grounds for divorce, like a wife killing their infant, wrecking their house or poisoning someone. He recognizes a husband might also be responsible for his wife's infidelity because he has failed to monitor the ways she associates with men or because he has refused to satisfy her sexual desires.

> And even he who withholds himself from his wife makes her oftentimes to be an adulteress when he does not satisfy her desires, even though he does so under the appearance of greater gravity and self-control. (XIV.24)

Before entering the Church, one of its key figures, St Augustine of Hippo (354–430), had a child by a woman he never married. After repenting of his youthful lust, Augustine elevated Christian marriage to the status of a sacrament – a visible sign of God's special blessing. He mentions this in *On the Good of Marriage* (*De Bono Conjugali*): 'marriage bears a certain sacramental character, can no way be dissolved but by the death of one of them' (Section 17). Augustine advises married couples to be moderate in satisfying the 'lusts of the flesh' and he allows for divorce for sexual unfaithfulness. But remarriage is off the agenda until a former spouse dies, as remarriage would be adultery and it would deny the wayward spouse the opportunity to repent and become reconciled.

Gradually, as the Church began to dominate Europe, Augustine's view of marriage as a sacrament and a lifelong unbreakable covenant prevailed. Through marriage, couples became one flesh – a single permanent unit. If one partner committed adultery, treated a spouse badly or deserted, the Church might agree to their living apart but they could not remarry.

Augustine's views continue to prevail in the Catholic Church. Those who divorce and then remarry outside the Catholic Church (and many do) while their former spouse is still alive are regarded by the Catholic Church as having committed the grave sin of adultery. They are not able to receive absolution for their sins through the sacraments of penance and communion. This could account for lower divorce rates in many Roman Catholic societies such as Ireland, Spain and Italy, and for the popularity of annulment rather than divorce among devout Roman Catholics. Nevertheless, annulment is difficult to obtain as it requires proving the marriage is invalid because it didn't meet legal or religious requirements or one of the partners acted in bad faith.

This means divorced and remarried Catholics are victims of not only a failed marriage but also their Church's condemnation and excommunication for taking a new partner. The only way out for the remarried partner is if the new partner dies or the couple separate, confess to their adultery and promise not to cohabit again.

The Catholic Church is criticized for sticking with a particular fourth-century theology, being overly legalistic, unforgiving and unjustly harsh on those who suffer a marriage failure, especially those who are the 'innocent' party who worked hard to hold the marriage together. Their treatment of the divorced is similar to the way in which lepers were treated in Jesus' time. Their leprosy was thought to be the result of sin, yet Jesus healed them (Mark 1.40–43; Luke 17.12–19). In practice, though, many Roman Catholic clergy and lay Catholics take a more understanding approach to divorced people than the official position would suggest.

The Protestant reformers looked back in the Bible to God's intention for marriage and often took a more liberal view of divorce. The great German reformer, Martin Luther (1483–1546), thought that treating marriage as a sacrament was a mockery and he was in two minds over the question of divorce. He stated in his *Of Matrimony*, 'I, for my part, detest divorce, and even prefer bigamy to it; but whether it be lawful I dare not define.' Nevertheless, he considered as grounds for divorce adultery, impotency and refusing to have sex with one's spouse, or abandoning one's spouse and family. He also accepted remarriage for the offended party. Other Protestant leaders added criteria such as threat to life and insanity. In all cases, fault had to be proved.

In his *The Judgement of Martin Bucer Concerning Divorce*, the lesser-known reformer, Martin Bucer (1491–1551), disagrees with the main purpose of marriage being sex and offspring. He says God requires married couples 'to live together, and to be united not only in body but in mind also, with such an affection as none may be dearer and more ardent among all the relations of mankind, nor of more efficacy to the mutual offices of love and loyalty'. He recommends that the irreconcilable breakdown of the marriage, whether from adultery, desertion, impotency, a disease like leprosy, or madness was sufficient reason for divorce and remarriage. Divorce could be by mutual consent or even by the desire of one partner. 'Matrimony requires continual cohabitation and living together, unless the calling of God be otherwise evident; which union if the parties themselves disjoin either by mutual consent, or one against the other's will depart, the marriage is then broken.' His views were not generally accepted until modern times.

Although divorce was possible in Protestant societies, the process was usually difficult and very public. In Britain, those wanting a divorce had to face an examination in a Church court. If the Church agreed to the separation, then an Act of Parliament was necessary to grant the couple their divorce, enabling them to remarry.

In 1858, the role of the Church courts in divorce was abolished in Britain. Parliament gave power to secular courts to grant absolute divorces and the right to remarry when there was fault. Many other countries where the Protestant influence was strong, including the USA, adopted a similar approach until the middle of the twentieth century.

The list of acceptable faults varied depending on the country or state's legislation. Adultery was usually at the top of the list. But typical of other faults were incest or other sexual offences, desertion, chronic drunkenness or drug addiction, insanity, long-term imprisonment, impotence or constant denial of sex, inability or failure to provide for the family, and cruelty. Cruelty, which came to include emotional as well as physical abuse, was a common reason for wives seeking divorce.

The main advantage of the fault system was that it gave definite grounds for divorce while reinforcing marriage and family values. It also gave a spouse who wanted to stay in a marriage some bargaining rights. He or she could be uncooperative and use delaying tactics, refuse a divorce, hold out for more than 50 per cent of the couple's wealth or dictate child custody arrangements in exchange for agreeing to the divorce.

The fault system meant that even if both partners were responsible for the collapse of the marriage, one spouse usually became the 'innocent victim' who asked the court to award a divorce because of the 'guilt' of the partner. Intimate details of married life were publicly exposed and put under the magnifying glass as evidence from one's partner, neighbours, workmates and private detectives was paraded in court.

Sometimes couples who wanted to divorce because the love between them had gone cold would fabricate evidence to meet the fault criteria. A common method was to hire a 'call girl' and for the husband to fake sex with her in front of a witness or pose for incriminating photos. Some marriage lawyers also had a reputation for turning ordinary marital disagreements and differences into instances of mental cruelty. This made a mockery of the fault system.

Shame was attached to guilty partners for failing to meet family obligations but sometimes there was condemnation of spouses wanting the divorce for not standing by their man or woman. This deterred many from leaving unhappy relationships. Some remained married in name only, living alone or in a de facto relationship with new partners.

The fault system failed to recognize that in most cases marriage breakdown involved both partners. Nor did it recognize other reasons for a marriage failing.

Since the 1960s, no-fault divorce has been adopted by many Western societies, making it possible for one partner to obtain a divorce without proving fault. However, the couple may have to remain separated for a time to allow for the possibility of reconciliation, before a divorce becomes final and the couple are free to marry again. The division of the couple's assets is usually 50/50. Courts settle disputed child custody issues on a case-by-case basis. This has shifted the legal rights from the person who wants to stay to the person who wants to leave.

Since 1973, England and Wales have used a mixed system of fault and no-fault divorce. You may still seek a faults divorce if you can prove your partner has committed adultery, deserted you for at least two years (which rarely happens) or displayed unreasonable behaviour. Unreasonable behaviour is conduct that is very difficult to live with, like financial irresponsibility, constant drunkenness, violence or emotional neglect. If you want a no-fault divorce, you'll need to show you've separated for at least two years and you both consent to a divorce. If your partner doesn't want a divorce, then you'll have to remain separated for five years before you can divorce without his or her consent. This gives some rights to the person who wants to remain in the marriage and allows time for possible reconciliation. But it's also a way of punishing the spouse who wants to leave. The law doesn't allow divorces in the first year of marriage.

The divorce law is similar in Northern Ireland, except you have to remain married two years before you can divorce. In Scotland, there is no time limit on when you can divorce and a shorter separation applies: one year if you both consent and two years if your partner doesn't consent. Bizarrely, the Scottish Judge, Lord Wheatley, claimed in a judgement that for adultery to occur there must be 'physical contact with an alien and unlawful sexual organ'.

Despite strong opposition from the Catholic Church, in 1997 no-fault divorce laws came into effect in the Republic of Ireland. To obtain a divorce, a couple have to show they have lived apart for at least four of the past five years, that there's no reasonable prospect of reconciliation and that there's proper provision for spouses and children.

The Eastern Orthodox Church also believes marriage is a sacrament. Unlike the Catholic Church, though, the Orthodox allow divorce and remarriage for adultery and other serious faults, which are determined on a case-by-case basis. This could include lack of love or commitment to the marriage. Counselling and genuine reconciliation attempts must have been tried, and failed, before the Church recognizes a divorce. Orthodox churches allow a person to marry only three times, even if his or her partners die.

In 2002 the Church of England General Synod allowed divorced persons to marry again in church.

While you may be able to get a divorce without proving fault, we all know from listening to friends who have been through a break-up that fault is still lurking in our thinking as a moral force. Most, in fact, will regard themselves as victims of circumstances or their partner's faults.

No-fault divorce may remove blame in theory, but if someone walks out of a marriage without adequate reason, it will seem the cruellest of injustices to the one left behind.

How do you decide whether to stay or go?

The Catholic Church has remained steadfast in its opposition to divorce and remarriage, yet the Orthodox Church and most Protestant Churches allow for divorce and remarriage, reflecting changing attitudes and ethical standards within our society. The Bible also describes attitudes to marriage and divorce changing, such as dropping polygamy and concubines in favour of monogamy after the Exile, and Jesus insisting marriage shouldn't get in the way of the First Commandment to love God and serve his kingdom. The writers of the New Testament epistles present marriage as more than a private property contract. It's a relationship of love similar to that between Christ and his Church (Eph. 5.22–23).

Most of us reflect ethical standards similar to our society, especially on questions of pelvic theology – issues of sex and sexuality. This might mean taking a different point of view from the official position of your own Church, like the majority of Catholics in a US survey who agreed that divorce for reasons other than adultery is not a sin. It may also explain why the divorce rate among Christians is similar to that of the rest of the population. This raises questions of how we know what is right and what God wants for us?

Some Christians say that God has given a definite answer through the Bible or Church authorities. But, as we've seen, the Bible and different Churches present different views. And even if we do believe in one theological stance, does its being in the Bible or our Church's official position automatically make it right?

The way to test this is to ask: if God or the Church authorities command us to do something that is wrong, like killing a spouse, would that make it right? Of course not. What is ethically right or wrong doesn't depend on who says it or where it's written – including the Bible. Something is morally right or wrong for other reasons, like whether it is just and fair, or whether it will bring greater happiness or unhappiness. Even the most fundamentalist Christians who disagree with divorce, except for adultery, wouldn't endorse the biblical command that those who commit adultery should receive the death penalty.

That doesn't mean, though, that the Bible or Church authorities are irrelevant. Far from it. Our faith provides ethical principles, guidelines and precedents from the Bible and through our Church history and doctrines. It gives us historical perspective to decide what is right and to avoid making mistakes like those of the Crusaders, the Spanish Inquisitors and other fanatics. Similarly, we recoil at the excessive zeal of those church leaders who've directed wives to stay in violent marriages or insisted husbands have conjugal rights when their wives could suffer serious harm or death. Naturally, arguments and interpretations are going to differ between denominations and scholars, and between cultures, as much as they do for other ethical issues and in secular law.

That may seem confusing. Yet there is a parallel precedent in the way the Church has treated war. Despite Jesus' desecration of the Temple (John 2.13–17) and the disciples carrying swords (Luke 22.36–38; John 18.10), New Testament and Church teachings have been strongly anti-violence and pro-peace. Jesus didn't allow his disciples to take up the sword to defend him against those arresting him (Matt. 26.52) and he insisted on forgiving those who executed him (Luke 23.34). He even taught in his Sermon on the Mount that the peacemakers are blessed (Matt. 5.9). The early Church adhered to these teachings, but that began to change after the Roman Empire accepted Christianity as an official religion and Christians came to accept military solutions which had peace as the goal. In the Middle Ages, St Thomas Aquinas (*c.* 1225–74) produced his three principles of a just war:

1 War can only be waged by a sovereign or legitimate authority, not private individuals.
2 The war must be for a just cause.
3 The war must be for the advancement of what is good, or against evil.

Since then the Catholic Church has added:

1 War must be a last resort.
2 Only proportional force is to be used to right the wrong.

Although the Church is strongly against war and promotes peace, it recognizes that occasionally war is necessary when it's the lesser of two evils. Similarly, the Church is strongly in favour of couples staying married and does what it can to promote healthy marriages and reconciliation when married partners fall out with one another. But, as with a just war, divorce and the possibility of remarriage can be a better option than staying in a very bad marriage. The Church itself has split when reconciliation was not possible, when the Orthodox Church left in the eleventh century, and again, when the Protestant Churches, which rose during the Protestant Reformation that began in the sixteenth century, broke away.

When Jesus' disciples were criticized for breaking the strict rules of the Sabbath by eating heads of grain as they walked through the fields, Jesus responded by saying, 'The Sabbath was made for man, not man for the Sabbath' (Mark 2.27). It's the spirit of the law rather than the letter of the law that is important. He also told his listeners, 'I have come that they may have life, and have it to the full' (John 10.10). In other words, Jesus didn't come to make us miserable through keeping the letter of the law, especially if it's serving no good purpose, like a bad marriage. But that doesn't mean we have the freedom to do exactly what we want.

Principles for a just divorce

There's a difference between fulfilling legal requirements and ethical ones. Even if your partner has committed adultery, abandoned you for many years or you believe he or she has treated you badly, you may meet the legal requirements for ending your marriage. But is it right to do so? Most marriages go through tough patches, and at times, one or other partner may feel the urge to leave. And there are always lawyers who'll be happy to benefit from assisting you to get a divorce.

I believe there are principles for a just divorce, based on Christian principles, which provide ethical and spiritual guidelines similar to Just War principles, to help those in unhappy marriages decide whether to stay or go. These key principles, and what they mean for Christians, are:

1 The marriage has broken down for valid reasons. (The marriage isn't fulfilling the purpose for which God ordained it.)
2 Genuine attempts have been made to save the marriage and bring about a workable reconciliation. (Prayer, perseverance, forgiveness and openness to God's reconciling love are unable to heal the rift.)

3 The split gives you and others who are affected a better chance for long-term happiness than if you and your partner stayed together. (The kingdom of God and his will are better fulfilled by you leaving your partner.)

If you answer yes to these three principles and you decide to leave, then this fourth principle also applies:

4 The separation needs to be just, fair and cause no unnecessary distress. (The separation needs to be a witness to God's healing love for all.)

We'll be looking at each of these principles in detail over the next chapters. I'll also be providing research information, examples and tools to help make the crucial decision as to whether to stay or leave your marriage.

5

Justifiable breakdown

―――――•·•·•――――――

Valid reasons

For a marriage to have broken down for valid reasons – so that it is not fulfilling the purpose for which God ordained it – something needs to be very wrong with the relationship. Here are six key conditions that can strike at the very heart of a marriage and break the mutuality or bond between you:

1 There's failure to meet essential emotional needs.
2 There's critical lack of commitment.
3 There's serious lack of trust.
4 You and your partner have major value differences.
5 The relationship is very unfair.
6 There's serious abuse.

Although listed separately, these conditions often overlap. For example, someone may neglect the essential emotional needs of a partner because of a stronger and unfair commitment to a lover – and lie about it.

Let's look at each of these conditions in turn.

There's failure to meet essential emotional needs

We often point to lack of communication as the main reason for marriage breakdown. Yet, couples can still be relating well to each other as they head for the divorce court. Failing to meet essential emotional needs is the most common reason. It's also the most difficult to justify to yourself and to others as it raises questions about what is an essential emotional need, differences in emotional needs between partners and whether you ought to expect your partner to satisfy your needs. And what if your needs are only partially satisfied or one of you is satisfied but not the other?

In practice, failure to meet your essential emotional needs means you're feeling lonely and unloved within your relationship, which is contrary to God's purpose for marriage. Your marriage isn't allowing you to give and receive love, intimacy, affection, nurturing or support, or possibly even to fulfil a desire for children. Maybe you've drifted apart because you no longer have much in common, because your needs are now different from what they once were, or because you get more emotional satisfaction from other people and other activities to be bothered with your partner. Whatever the reason, your union as a couple – body, mind and heart – is not happening and may not have happened for years. The relationship you do have might be less like lovers and more like business partners sharing the same house.

This is a standard scenario. Often, though, the situation is not so straightforward. What if you and your partner have a good relationship in some ways, yet you get only 40 per cent of what you think you should reasonably expect from your relationship? Maybe your partner is a good person who works hard to create a comfortable home for you and your family but finds it hard to give or receive affection.

What if you both said you wanted a home full of kids when you were courting, yet your husband has convinced you to wait a while so you might have time to enjoy each other? Ten years later, he's still saying the same thing. He's enjoying being a DINK (double income, no kids). You've avoided a showdown on the issue but you now desperately want a child.

In cases like these, even though the marriage is satisfying in many ways, it's not fulfilling a key purpose. It would be different if you were both satisfied with the situation, like the growing number of couples who mutually decide not to have children because they believe they'll have greater freedoms, more money, a better relationship or because they don't want the responsibility of offspring.

It's only fair to share your frustration and suggest looking at ways to remedy the situation together. If your spouse has changed his or her mind and insists on not having children, you may need to remind him or her how important this is to you and, if necessary, give an ultimatum, especially if you're a woman concerned about your biological clock. If this fails, you may need to consider how else you can reach agreement, and, if that fails, you may have to face the possibility of leaving to find someone who can fulfil your needs.

If your partner is suffering from impotence, that could mean medical or psychological therapy. If your partner refuses, you may need to issue a warning that you expect him or her to undergo treatment and, if one treatment fails, to try another; otherwise, you'll have to reassess your relationship. In the unlikely event all reasonable attempts at treatment fail, then at least you will know your partner has done all that is possible to improve the relationship.

If you are unable to have children, then you may need to look at other options such as fertility treatments, artificial insemination or adoption.

What if you're desperate for a third child and your partner reckons that two is enough? As frustrating as this may be, is it grounds for leaving? Or is it a question of changing expectations? You're not always going to get your own way or all your emotional needs satisfied by your partner. And you won't always be able to satisfy your partner's needs. Most happily married couples find they are fulfilled most of the time and can find a way to work out differences like the need for more affection or sex, or whether or not to have a third child. If you can't sort out these differences, it could indicate there's a major difference in values (see below: 'You and your partner have major value differences', p. 66).

A common complaint is how the partner of your youth no longer meets the changed needs of your later years. Perhaps your kids have left the nest and you've both retired from regular employment. You realize you no longer have much in common. While you planned to stay together until parted by death, the passion and affection has gone and the relationship seems to have served its purpose. Surveys show that a significant number of married women, in particular, would not marry the man they are currently married to if they had the chance of choosing again, and usually it's the woman who instigates leaving when she feels emotionally deprived.

This was the scenario of Mike and Lisa, mentioned in Chapter 1, pp. 9–11. Mike felt that although the relationship could be better, it was acceptable, whereas Lisa felt bored, neglected and unhappy. After marriage counselling failed, Lisa decided to leave even though Mike pleaded with her to stay.

If your emotional needs are not satisfied, is that sufficient reason for wanting to leave? After all, love is not a life-and-death necessity like food, water, clothing, shelter or basic security. While undoubtedly frustrated, many couples do stay together as friends who benefit financially and socially from living in the same home.

In such a situation, sublimating your needs by submerging yourself in other people and activities may work for a time but you may well decide that only a loving partner can make you happy again.

Many seek a lover to fill the emotional gap. If you do break the Seventh Commandment, there'll be the initial excitement of the honeymoon stage of a new relationship, with the added allure of the risqué. The honeymoon glow of the affair may transfer to your marriage and reawaken the passion, but it will also emphasize to you what's wrong. You may face guilt, possible ill health, conflicts of loyalty and questions about your character and Christian commitment because of the broken trust and deception. It could also hasten the end of your marriage.

Your lover may act as a catalyst to show what's missing from your marriage and what you need to do. But what about your responsibilities to your lover? He or she may have hoped for something more from your relationship and you might have encouraged that hope. Is this the risk your lover takes? Maybe. But you need to take his or her feelings into consideration too.

Sometimes your needs aren't met because you and your partner are parted from each other for long periods. Maybe one of you is imprisoned or hospitalized for many years, you spend long periods apart because of work or you've agreed to live separate lives.

In situations like these, it's a matter of finding out over a reasonable period whether there's enough emotional bonding to fulfil your needs through visits, letters, emails and telephone calls. You might be the kind of people who enjoy your independence or don't need intimacy as much as others. Absence could make your hearts grow fonder.

Nevertheless, those who are happy with a remote relationship are the exception. You're more likely to feel that such a relationship is a denial of the companionship and intimacy you expect and need from the marriage. It's a hardship you can expect to endure faithfully for only a few years.

If your partner abandons you or you don't want to make the effort to keep the relationship going, then you have, in effect, separated as a couple.

Whether you choose to stay or leave will depend largely on your answers to the second and third principles of whether there's anything you can do to save the marriage and whether there's likely to be greater long-term happiness if you leave.

In the case of Monica and Gerard, outlined in Chapter 1, pp. 8 9, who had been married 22 years when Monica was diagnosed with the degenerative and fatal Alzheimer's disease, the relationship was no longer able to meet either of their needs. Monica was hospitalized and could no longer remember her family, let alone have a meaningful relationship with them. Gerard was doing all that a husband could do under the circumstances and he was determined to continue to manage her care until death. But he also needed to move on with his life and it was reasonable he should be free to marry his new partner without waiting out Monica's prognosis of further degeneration and death within eight years.

Researchers might discover a miracle cure for Alzheimer's and reverse the disease's progress in Monica. But how likely is that to happen? Even if a potential miracle drug or medical procedure is found, it normally takes years of trials before it's deemed safe. On the off chance of the remote possibility of a miracle cure, it would be severely unfair on Gerard and his new partner to expect them to wait.

What if your basic emotional needs are met, yet you feel your relationship cramps your potential?

In 1943, psychologist Abraham Maslow published his popular theory of human motivation. Maslow stacks our needs in their order of importance. At the bottom are basic physiological needs; followed by security needs; then love, belonging and self-esteem needs. Once these needs are met, we're free to become all we can be. Maslow calls this self-actualization. The musician is able to play music and the writer to write. In simple terms, it means being able to do what really energizes and fulfils you.

In contrast to Lisa who left because her emotional needs were not being met in her marriage, 39-year-old Angie dreamed of a life of self-fulfilment unencumbered by the drudgery of home and husband and open to romance, travel and all those lifestyle choices she had never been able to make because of putting her family first for 18 years. She took a holiday abroad alone, and when she returned energized, she joined a gym and took up courses in interior design. The change alarmed her husband, Kevin, and their two teenage children. When they accused her of being selfish, it only added to Angie's dissatisfaction.

Friends told her she was suffering a mid-life crisis, and while they admitted Kevin was unexciting, they reminded her that he was kind, gentle, on a good income – and he hadn't done anything to hurt her.

Angie argued back, 'If it's OK to get married for romantic ideals, then it's OK to leave for romantic ideals. I'd rather risk all and leave at this stage than lose the opportunity and regret it later in life.'

History is full of stories of adventurers, inventors, artists, missionaries like St Peter (whom we are told had a mother-in-law [Mark 1.30], so must assume he had a wife), and others who would never have achieved what they did, or gained fame, if they hadn't cast their relationships aside to fulfil a burning passion. However, the key test here involves the third principle, discussed in detail in Chapter 8, p. 104, of whether the split will create greater long-term happiness for all affected than if they stayed.

Angie's dream of becoming an interior designer came to nothing and she took a low-paying job as a shop assistant. Although she did meet new people, she also attracted men she described as 'creepy and only after one thing'. Most nights she watched television or read alone in her flat. She saw much less of her children, who even though they still loved her, blamed her for complicating their lives. Instead of becoming self-actualized, Angie was now struggling to meet basic needs. Her self-esteem had taken a knock, but even though Kevin wanted her to give their marriage another chance and was willing to help her establish a business, her pride wouldn't let her go back on her decision.

No one benefited from Angie leaving Kevin. Their relationship might seem duller than reading last year's weather forecasts, but it hadn't broken down. Perhaps she was blaming it for holding her back instead of finding ways to liven it up and still achieve what she most needed to do without leaving Kevin.

There's a critical lack of commitment

There are times when it is right for one partner to direct more time and energy to parents or children, or to give work commitments priority. It's when your partner's loyalty continues to remain much stronger to others than to you that the marriage fails. Your partner no longer wants to forsake all others for you. That may include a lover.

According to British surveys, nearly 20 per cent of married men and 13 per cent of married women have had an affair. About one-in-seven married men visit a prostitute, whereas only a small percentage of married women pay for sex. In street ministry as a priest, I learned from sex workers that many married men hire someone to fulfil sexual needs that aren't met at home but go on to spend much of their time talking, hugging and fulfilling emotional needs. The prostitute is a companion and counsellor in a non-judgemental environment.

When confronted with an extramarital affair, unfaithful spouses often plead, as Steve did to Sue in the case of infidelity mentioned in Chapter 1, pp. 5–7, 'It was only sex. It didn't mean anything.' They are admitting that it was wrong to forget love and commitment, even temporarily, and to succumb to temptation. They now want forgiveness, and as Christianity is about forgiveness and love, that needs to be seriously considered.

Infidelity is, of course, very difficult to cope with. A British study found there's more than a 50 per cent chance a marriage will end after an affair. Often that's because the partner who has the affair knowingly or subconsciously wants to end the marriage. It's as if he or she is expecting the spouse to pick up the clues and learn of the infidelity. So the offending spouse has, in effect, handed their spouse the moral and legal grounds for ending the marriage.

Steve thought having a guilty secret gnawing at his conscience would be more harmful to their marriage. Would it have been better if he'd kept quiet?

This is a difficult one. If you're in this position, ask yourself whether you honestly want to save your marriage. If you're confused, it may be worth talking first to a counsellor or a wise and discreet friend who will help you sort out how you really feel. It certainly isn't worth telling your spouse if he or she is likely to react with violence or threaten you or your lover's safety. Even if you decide never to tell your spouse or to wait for several months or years before you mention your indiscretion, try to answer any questions your partner asks as honestly as you can. Otherwise, you'll end up entangling yourself in your own web of deceit and half-truths. This may prove more damaging to the trust that underpins your relationship than the affair, especially if your partner finds out about your clandestine love life that you were trying to conceal.

If you decide to tell, wait for when he or she is ready to listen. Be prepared for an emotional reaction. Although your partner may have suspected the affair, your confession may still come as a shock and his or her initial reaction could be similar to Sue's. Tell the truth and take responsibility for your actions. Don't try to justify your infidelity or blame your spouse's faults or your lover's virtues and seductive powers. Resist claiming that any guilt pangs you're suffering are punishment for your indiscretion.

Make it clear you've given up your lover and describe the measures you're taking to avoid further temptation. Work with your partner on developing ways to move beyond the effects of the affair to a better partnership. Identify what drove you into the arms of your lover and find other ways of meeting these needs. Seek counselling if this will help.

What would you do if your wife confessed she's pregnant after a fling with your best mate, who was last seen heading for the airport?

An angry husband raised that question on a New Zealand radio talk show. He wanted his distraught spouse to 'abort or walk', and as she didn't believe in abortion, she was going to become a twice-abandoned solo mother. That set the switchboard ablaze for several days as listeners shared experiences and gave advice. Then the show's host asked me for a concluding comment.

At least the wife was honest. DNA testers at Liverpool's John Moores University found that 1 in 25 men is bringing up another man's child – and doesn't know it. But I did point out that, because of her honesty, her husband would face the consequences of his wife and friend's unfaithfulness every day if they stayed together and she had the child. I also reminded him that plenty of men and women marry each other when they already have children by previous relationships and to ask himself whether he would have married his wife if he'd met her when she was pregnant. He might well have. What mattered most was where her heart was, and it was clearly with him.

As Christians, we believe in forgiveness and reconciliation. That's our intention, but our feelings can defy the best of intentions. So, it could take several difficult years to restore your partner's confidence and trust. Consider whether it's worth staying in your marriage if, despite determined efforts at reconciliation, you find that there's no basis for trust between you, there's no will to forgive, you don't want to give up your extramarital relationship(s) or you continue to be very unhappy in your marriage.

What if you're the one who's faithful and you catch your partner and a lover together *in flagrante delicto*? Of course, you'll feel utterly devastated. Yet, even though your partner has betrayed your trust and loyalty, and the lover could be a friend who has also betrayed you, try to avoid issuing ultimatums in the heat of the moment. Forcing your spouse to choose between you and a lover or announcing that your marriage is over could force an outcome that's difficult to reverse if it isn't what you really want. It's probably best to walk away from the situation until you can digest what's happened and then at an appropriate time listen to what your partner has to say. Establish how committed you and your partner are to staying together. If you do want to stay together, come up with positive ways in which you can both put the affair behind you and avoid infidelity in the future.

A one-night stand or a short affair may not be sufficient reason for ending the marriage. As painful as it may be, it is likely to bring to the surface underlying problems and unfulfilled needs which can at last be worked through honestly by you as a couple, maybe with the help of a marriage counsellor.

A longstanding affair, in contrast, implies more than an indiscretion. Even if your unfaithful spouse insists you're his or her true love and favourite partner, you are, in effect, sharing your marriage bed with another. If your partner continues with the adultery, it shows a lack of commitment that would be grounds to consider ending the marriage.

A partner acting as if he or she is still single is another example of lack of commitment. Perhaps he or she treats your home like a hotel – a place to eat and sleep and watch TV – and ignores you most of the time.

Beliefs and interests in common usually help to create a better marriage. But your partner may become overly preoccupied with a belief, a cause, a special interest or career to the detriment of your relationship. When this happens, you'll feel neglected and forsaken for another.

Whether the marriage can be salvaged will depend on how determined you both are to committing yourselves to each other. If your own attempts, the intervention of friends and relatives, counselling, prayer and other efforts to change attitudes and lifestyle for the sake of the relationship fail, then you may need to give your partner an ultimatum to change or you'll leave. Otherwise, you'll need to conclude that your relationship is no longer the union of two people operating as one flesh.

There's a serious lack of trust

Trust can be shattered the instant you learn your spouse is deliberately deceiving you, especially over something you personally regard as significant. One distressed woman told me how she was suspicious when she found shredded paper in the family rubbish. Nancy showed me the results of her painstaking work taping the pieces together. It was a bank statement containing regular payments from her husband's employer to a personal account in his name. The bank was in a tax-free island state and the account contained a large sum of money.

'I confronted Harry with this and asked him what was going on', Nancy explained. 'He looked me straight in the eye and said, "I wanted it to be a surprise. I was going to buy that dream home you always wanted for us." But that doesn't explain why an off-shore bank account and why he lied to me about how much money he was making. Even if his story is true and he was doing it for good motives, I still feel betrayed. He was deciding what to do with the money instead of consulting with me.'

Nancy's trust in Harry kept being eroded, especially after she told him that she was perfectly happy with their current home and he refused to consider transferring the money to their joint account: 'He keeps giving these excuses, like we need to have the money for a rainy day or it makes it easier for paying taxes, which makes me suspicious about what else he's up to behind my back. I want to trust him, but I can't.'

Your spouse may lie or not tell the whole truth to protect you from distress, such as not wanting you to know he or she has a terminal illness, or deception may be a requirement of a top-secret job. But these cases are rare. Cheating usually involves trying to gain a personal advantage through hiding criminal, unethical, addictive or embarrassing behaviour and then lying about it.

Your partner might also tell you one thing and say or do the opposite behind your back, like undermining your standing with friends and family with malicious gossip.

Often the shock of uncovering the deception is worse than what's been concealed, though once everything's out in the open there's the opportunity for both of you to heal any misunderstanding or unhappiness and a chance for regrets and apologies to be made. In the same way that Peter learned from his denial of Jesus (Mark 14.37–38, 66–72), the relationship can be repaired and strengthened.

If the disloyal or deceitful behaviour continues, however, trust is difficult to maintain. To avoid detection again, your partner may become more devious – and you'll become more astute at detection. You'll wonder how your partner can possibly continue to love you when he or she constantly lies, cheats or steals. A basic element of loyalty is missing.

This is what happened with Harry and Nancy mentioned above. Nancy suspected Harry of stashing his money in a secret offshore account so he wouldn't have to pay alimony when he left her, which she was now certain he was going to do. And Harry reacted to Nancy's distrust by becoming more secretive and moving his money to a new offshore account. Their mutual mistrust grew to the point where Nancy told Harry she was thinking of leaving him.

Your partner's shock at learning you're thinking of splitting may help to turn the situation around. So may the intervention of others, including the efforts of a counsellor. This is what happened with Nancy and Harry, whose issues were more to do with love of money than lack of love for Nancy. But if the trust between you has gone and can't be resurrected, the marriage has broken down.

You and your partner have major value differences

It can be very difficult to maintain a relationship when you and your partner have different core values: life goals, ethics, religious convictions, political and ideological beliefs, the use of money, the upbringing of children and your daily lifestyle.

How you respond to these differences will depend on how strongly each of you holds your convictions and values. If you're a devout Christian and your partner is a non-believer, then your partner may come to resent the time and energy you spend at church and doing outreach work. The situation could become even more difficult if your spouse is an atheist actively opposing what you believe.

Is it worth compromising on fundamental beliefs? For those of us who are committed to our Christian faith, that would be asking too much. We can love and respect our partner and still disagree with his or her point of view. But Jesus makes it clear that he expects us to be totally committed, forsaking anything that stands in the way of following him – including wealth and family ties. As was discussed in Chapter 4, p. 43, one of the reasons Christians should stay married to unbelievers is so their lives can be a witness to their spouses in the hope that they will come to embrace the faith. And this does sometimes happen: several of my clergy friends have spouses who've eventually joined the Church after spending most of their married lives as agnostics.

But how long should you stay married to a partner who constantly ridicules and disrespects your faith? Should you do as St Paul recommends (1 Cor. 7.12–16) and stay until your unbelieving partner leaves you? Jesus warned, 'Do not give dogs what is sacred; do not throw your pearls to pigs' (Matt. 7.6), and told his disciples not to hang about in places where their message wasn't received (Mark 6.11). Similarly, if requests to your partner to respect your faith are ignored, then consider counselling and, if that fails, think about separation as a serious option. While we are asked to be faithful witnesses and to take up our cross daily, that doesn't mean we should stay in an abusive relationship.

Even if you've compromised for the meantime, questions of which faith to bring your children up in, whether to baptize them and what kind of school or religious education they should have could divide you and your spouse later on.

Fights over money loom large in many homes. One of you might believe in giving a percentage of your income to a church or charity and the other may believe it's better to spend it on much-needed items for the home. One might gamble money on high-risk ventures while the other wants to take a more conservative approach. One may want to quit work to study for a qualification while the other may feel that this isn't worth the drop in standard of living, and so on.

How you think about your money represents your different goals and convictions. If giving to church and charities is part of your strongly held faith, you may not want to compromise. Your partner may, of course, see this as squandering joint funds and consider it a reason for leaving you. You may, or may not, find middle ground.

Similarly, if the job you're doing is deadly dull and frustrating to you, studying for a qualification that will give you a more interesting and challenging career will be of utmost importance. You'll need to convince your partner of how this will benefit your future relationship. And if you can't, then the relationship may face a breakdown.

What if you learn your partner's a drug dealer or believes it's okay to defraud customers? The question becomes even more critical if your partner implicates you or the family in his or her bad behaviour. Could you help your partner in these activities? If this goes against your core beliefs, you might distance yourself by adopting an attitude of 'that's got nothing to do with me and our relationship'. But it does, and most of us would react to such a serious character flaw in our partner by trying to get him or her to change. If your partner doesn't want to change or efforts to do so fail, then you'd have to weigh up whether you want to remain with a partner who continues to act immorally and illegally.

Although we adapt to one another's expectations and differences, few of us want to compromise the integrity of our character or what we believe is fundamentally right. Furthermore, no one else can expect us to compromise on what is basic to who we are and what we believe. That's because it means changing core beliefs and acting out of character. If your core beliefs and values are so incompatible as to be a perpetual stumbling block, that means the relationship has broken down.

The relationship is very unfair

Couples are different. What works for you and your partner may not work for another couple. In some relationships the wife is the homemaker and the husband earns the living, in others these gender roles are reversed, and in many, both may go to work and share the chores. Some Christians follow the advice of St Paul to treat the husband as the head of the household, whom the wife and children obey (Eph. 5.22; Col. 3.18). Nevertheless, whatever style of partnership you have, if your partner's needs, interests or influence constantly dominate the relationship or you're bullied into acting as an unwilling servant to your spouse's self-centeredness, then it's unfair. It's no longer a mutual relationship. You've become a minor partner, the insignificant other.

Naturally, there's self-interest in any relationship. At times your needs will dominate and at other times it will be your partner's needs. But when the scales constantly and very definitely tip one way, the relationship is unfair.

Maybe your spouse is convinced you have an obligation to support him or her. Possibly he or she competes against you and stacks the odds so that you lose. Maybe you're treated like a parent who's expected to look after your partner as if he or she were a spoilt child. Your spouse might consider he or she is more deserving through bringing more wealth and assets into the marriage, earning more or working longer hours.

What about the partner who demands the right to overrule your experience and judgement, taking control of your finances, the children's education, the family vehicle, or the TV remote? Even if your partner listens to your demands for a fairer deal, your needs and views are usually treated with condescension. While he or she may have expertise and good judgement in some things, that is no excuse to treat you with contempt and bullying behaviour.

Bullying may also take the form of restricting who you can have as friends, when you can leave the house and what you can say to people.

Julia's husband, Tom, was proud that he had a young attractive wife. But he was also jealous of the attention she received from other men and made sure she met only women friends, and not other men or couples if he wasn't present. He limited what Julia could talk about in mixed company so she wouldn't overshadow him or encourage undue attention from men. If she broke the rules merely out of social politeness, he reprimanded her and withheld money, the use of the car and the telephone. In contrast, Tom met with whomsoever he pleased, including single women.

While cultural customs for the way men and women relate to each other vary widely within any society, Tom's behaviour was well beyond the accepted norms of our western social order. He dominated and bullied Julia for fear of losing her. His insecurity denied the equality of their union and forced Julia to operate according to a standard beyond his own. Tom provided a climate in which what he was trying to avoid would be likely to happen. Julia tried to convince Tom to give her greater freedom and promised him that she would never stray or say anything that she thought would embarrass or shame him. But her pleas were to no avail. After separating from Tom temporarily several times, Julia finally left him and, within a year, was living with someone else. For Tom, this was proof of why he'd needed to keep a tight rein on her, whereas Julia felt she was now with a man who respected and treated her as a true equal.

The promise to stay with each other for better or for worse seems straightforward. It's easy during the better times, but even if things take a turn for the worse you accept it's about supporting each other through the crisis. Usually, this is for a limited period.

But what if your partner now has a disability or psychiatric disorder and depends on you? You have to spend a considerable amount of your time, energy and the family resources looking after him or her. You might have tried all possible solutions, including alternative medicine, but to little avail. You're very aware that your marriage is for better or for worse, yet the relationship is no longer a fair one. Even if help's available to ease the burden, should you stay?

It depends on whether the marriage is still viable. For Monica with Alzheimer's disease and Gerard, mentioned in Chapter 1, pp. 8–9, the marriage was viable in name only and continuing to stay married was unfair on Gerard's new partner, who wanted to be a wife rather than a mistress.

Leonard and Joan's situation is more difficult. For the past 15 of their 25 years together, Joan had suffered from a bipolar psychiatric disorder. At times she had high energy accompanied by bursts of intellectual activity and creativity. Sometimes she acted recklessly. She invited strangers into their home to drink with her while Leonard was at work, gave away their possessions and drove the family car recklessly. But most of the time, Joan was lethargic, suffered from mild depression and drank alone from supplies of liquor she had hidden all round the house.

Leonard's job and income supported the family. The housework and care of their two children also fell on him. Joan responded well to treatment but didn't always take her medication as she believed the pills poisoned her mind. She accused Leonard of having an affair with every woman he met and refused to recognize she suffered from an alcohol problem.

As their youngest child was about to leave home for work overseas, Leonard wondered whether it was time to seek a divorce. 'Although there have been good times and we have two wonderful kids, I can't continue to act the housekeeper, nurse and security guard, trying to protect Joan from herself. Joan's sickness dominates our relationship', he argued. 'Her condition has seriously affected my job and our quality of life. I love Joan but it's hell living with her. How long must I accept this before I'm morally free to leave?'

Leonard's well-meaning friends gave him plenty of conflicting advice. It ranged from, 'I don't know how you've put up with the situation for so long. You've gone more than the second mile' to 'Joan depends on you. Marriage is for life and when one partner falls, it's the duty of the other to help. Wouldn't you expect her to stay with you and help you?'

Where mental incapacity is recognized as grounds for divorce, as it is in some states and countries, Leonard may be justified in leaving after several years. Similarly, imprisonment or hospitalization for more than two years (depending on the laws that apply) might also be grounds for divorce. The implication here is that 'for better or for worse' applies to a temporary rather than an enduring condition which creates an unfair burden for the other spouse. So, the comment that Leonard had gone the extra mile for Joan and that he could leave with moral impunity would be fair under such a system.

But Leonard needed to live with his conscience. The key question he had to ask himself was whether the marriage was still viable, despite the disadvantages. For some people, the answer is 'yes' even though there are considerable hardships. For them, there are enough plusses to make it worthwhile. For most, though, the marriage has broken down.

Leonard wavered, concerned that Joan would deteriorate or take her own life if he left, but eventually, after arranging for her living needs, he left. Surprisingly, the shock of the separation made Joan desperate to win Leonard back. She took her medication, went to Alcoholics Anonymous, did volunteer church work and tried hard to act responsibility. Her sustained determination had its effect on Leonard. They came back together, and although Joan did have temporary lapses, their relationship was born again.

There's serious abuse

Arguments get volatile in some marriages. Insults are exchanged, doors slammed, dishes thrown, a partner withdraws until the anger subsides. Often such heated exchanges clear the air. Even so, constant insults and violence against doors, vases and dishes can be intimidating and traumatic. We don't need to resort to such dramatic and symbolic shows every time we have a difference.

While some couples spice up their sex lives with bondage and sado-masochistic behaviour such as whipping and using foul language, establishing mutually agreed boundaries under these circumstances is vital. Quite apart from the threat to personal safety, violence in the marriage bed, even if done in fun, may lead to violence in other areas of the relationship.

The line is crossed when your own or your family's safety is threatened. Even if you believe you have a Christian duty to obey your spouse, marriage isn't a licence for your partner to use you as a punch-bag, sex slave or someone on whom to vent his or her frustrations and anger. Nor does it permit anyone to abuse other members of the family in this way. You may be dependent upon your partner for money and other necessities, but that's no reason to accept abuse. Perhaps he or she needs you, but staying, even for the sake of the kids, provides further opportunity for your spouse to harm you or provoke you to act against your better nature.

There are organizations and agencies listed in the telephone directory and on the internet which can help if you're suffering from family violence.

The threat of violence doesn't have to be a physical one. It may be against something you value or an act of sabotage against your family home, your vehicle, your savings or your work. For example, if your partner destroys all your essential business records, you, your customers and suppliers could suffer financial hardship.

Humiliation and emotional abuse are as damaging as any other form of assault against you. Insults, swearing, crudeness, viciousness, put-downs, disdain, ridicule, threats and other disrespectful behaviour can be just as menacing and harmful as physical abuse. So, too, can your partner constantly grilling you as if you're an enemy agent, which is what Tom did to Julia whenever he thought she had talked to a man behind his back. Deborah's story is another example of the extreme emotional abuse that about 5 per cent of spouses suffer from their partners.

As my husband, Andy, walked in the door, he shouted, 'What's for dinner, slut?' No matter what I gave him, he swore it was shit and he wouldn't give it to the dog. He was even worse about my performance in bed. If I made a real effort, he called me a whore. If I refused him anything, I was a frigid bitch. He never hit me but I dreaded his coming home from work and I was constantly sick.

Andy scoffed when Deborah suggested counselling and insisted she was the one with the problem. As a devout Christian, Deborah believed this was the daily cross Jesus promised (Mark 8.34) and she had a duty to turn the other cheek and forgive her husband (Matt. 5.39). But her attitude produced a counter-reaction in Andy. He accused her of 'acting like a sanctimonious bitch and martyr'.

Forgiving others, though, doesn't mean putting ourselves in a position where we allow them to abuse us continually. It means giving them the opportunity to change their behaviour, and if there's a lapse when they revert to old ways we forgive and encourage them to recovery through the grace of God. If that fails, we need to take steps to remove ourselves from the abusive situation before the constant indignity undermines our confidence and leads to stress-related disorders or depression.

Some couples go through a cycle where one partner abuses the other, then becomes remorseful and pleads forgiveness. They then go through a period of making up, which is intense and romantic. This behaviour easily becomes addictive.

What made Deborah's plight so extreme was that Andy made no effort to apologize or make up. There were no temporary rewards. She came to the slow realization that if there is no solution to your partner dominating you the marriage has broken down.

Andy was shocked when she left him. He assumed that in their co-dependent relationship she needed him as much as he needed a wife to dominate and abuse. It took many years before Deborah regained her confidence and trusted herself with another man, but her husband soon remarried and repeated his abusive behaviour.

Even when his second wife left him, he continued to deny that he had a problem or that therapy might help.

Sometimes abuse is the result of an addiction, psychiatric disorder or other medical condition. If this is the case, therapy may be able to control or even cure the condition.

Some partners threaten to hurt themselves. It might be to gain your attention or to blackmail you so that they can get their own way. Alternatively, your partner could be suicidal and you find yourself carrying a burden of responsibility. The question you need to answer is whether your partner will respond to treatment. If not, and your staying increases the threat of harm, then your relationship is a threat to your partner. The marriage has broken down.

What if you're so unhappy with your marriage that you're thinking of suicide or some other violent action against yourself? Perhaps you feel that as you promised to stay married until parted by death, you ought to sacrifice yourself and set your partner free to get on with his or her life. If you're at this point and have been for some time, then you have all the more reason to consider leaving the marriage – but not in a coffin.

6

Has your marriage broken down?

Evidence

Even if you think your marriage has broken down, you may still hope it will come right. What if your partner had a different job or you had a baby? Maybe if one of you won a lottery, the relationship would improve. What if a new wonder drug could treat your partner's medical condition? Then again, maybe through loving perseverance and the power of prayer you will win over your partner. There are plenty of 'ifs'.

And there's evidence to support these hopes. During the late 1980s, University of Chicago sociologist Linda Waite and her team interviewed 645 adults who said they were unhappily married. Five years later, these unhappy partners were re-interviewed. Nearly a quarter had separated or divorced, and of these, about a half said they were happy. Of the majority of the originally unhappy spouses who stayed married, two-thirds said their marriages were now happy. Those who rated their marriages as very unhappy reported the most dramatic turnaround. Almost 80 per cent said they were happily married five years later.

So prayer, hope and working at your marriage can work. This is most likely to happen if you're both willing to recognize there's something wrong, and you both want to make it succeed and are pre-pared to modify annoying behaviour and make compromises. The support of family, friends and members of your church community is also important in reinforcing how special your relationship is. The research by Linda Waite and her team also suggests that unless there's a serious threat of harm, it's worth waiting several years before deciding there's no hope for your marriage.

Nevertheless, living in hope year after year as the relationship deteriorates despite your own best efforts to make it work and umpteen prayers, can be like continuing to buy lottery tickets in the hope of winning a major prize. It can happen but the chances are slim.

The question of how and where to draw the line on your marriage boils down to what's reasonable and what's God's will.

Are your intentions honest?

How honest are your intentions? We get more sympathy and can feel justified if we are convinced we're the victims of our partner's bad behaviour or that we weren't suited for each other in the first place. So you'll be tempted to blame, make excuses and select evidence that supports acceptable reasons for quitting. And as all relationships have their share of conflicts and difficulties, you'll be able to point, as evidence, to plenty of negative things your partner does and says.

Provoking your partner to do something that gives you the moral high ground is another motive of which to be aware if you know your partner's strengths and weaknesses and how to rouse him or her to abuse, drinking or drug binges, to neglect of you or the family, to unfaithfulness or some other form of negative behaviour. Your partner may need to accept responsibility for his or her own behaviour, but you do too.

And there's always the possibility that lurking on the dark side of your personality is an angry desire to punish your partner with a preemptive strike.

You need to be aware of your intentions and how these can cause you to select evidence that fits what you want. Take a look at the wider picture with the help of wise people who know you and your relationship or who have skills to get you to examine your motives.

Assessing whether there's a breakdown

The Relationship assessment (Table 6.1) is a prompt to help you reflect on the state of your marriage and become more aware of your intentions by asking you to look at what you think are the positive and negative aspects of your relationship, how you react to them, how strongly you feel about them and how you would rank them in order of importance.

Instructions

Set up two tables: one for the positive and the other for the negative aspects of the relationship, as shown in the example of Jenny's answers below. This enables you to compare the good with the bad.

Once you've set up your columns and rows, ask God to guide you to answer honestly. Then imagine you're a news reporter looking at your situation and try to jot down objectively a few key words and phrases that sum up what has been going on. Focus on significant events as well as recurring behavioural patterns, comments and feelings.

It's worth limiting yourself to three key answers for each question. This helps focus on what you think is important. If you change your mind and think of a different answer later, decide which is the least important of your answers and, if necessary, replace a previous answer with the new one.

If you find this difficult, consider filling in the tables with the help of a wise friend, a trusted member of your parish or a professional counsellor. Try to be honest. Don't try to please – or to shock.

Guide to filling in the Relationship assessment tables

Positive and negative

In the 'Positive aspects of the relationship' assessment table, note what's most positive about the relationship, and in the 'Negative aspects of the relationship' assessment table, note what's negative. Consider how you share your faith, values and attitudes, how you communicate, as well as your intellectual, emotional and physical, social and economic, and work and family life together.

Response

Jot down how you respond to your partner. It can help you understand how you may contribute to your partner's reactions to you.

Feelings

Your feelings are vital to your decision. Feelings may include happiness, desire, distress, sadness, grief, anger, guilt, fear, anxiety, concern, confidence, uncertainty, pain, moodiness, depression, pride, shame, jealousy, envy, nausea, lethargy, disappointment, repugnance or loathing – to name the more common ones. Are there contradictions like enjoying your spouse's intellect and humour but despairing of his or her emotional detachment?

Comment

Note comments that explain why. They cast light on what's happening. A remark about why the conversations are great, yet you feel anxious, might include the observation: 'It's an intellectual relationship that has little intimacy.'

Impact on you

This enables you to score the points you raise. The score ranges from −2 if the impact on you is bad or very negative, −1 if the impact is somewhat bad, 0 if the impact is neutral through to +1 if it is somewhat good, and +2 if the impact is good or very positive.

Jenny's sample answers below are a guide as to how to set up and fill out your own table. You'll have different experiences from those in the sample, so your answers will be different.

Ranking

Rank all your answers for both tables combined as to how significant they are to you. Score what matters most with 1 and what matters least with 18. You can rate two or more answers at the same level. If you note that you 'both like the same type of music', that is likely to be less important than if you mention 'dismissive and hurtful comments'.

Reviewing your answers

When you've filled out the two tables put them aside. About once a week over the next two months ask for God's guidance, review what

Table 6.1 Relationship assessment: Jenny's sample answers

a Positive aspects of the relationship

Question	Positives	Your response	Your feelings	Comment	Impact on you −2 = bad +2 = good	Ranking (both tables) 1 ⊃ 18
1 What do you find appealing about your partner?	Good to talk to on an intellectual and humorous level.	Chat as an equal.	Intellectually stimulated.	About the only thing that's still working as it doesn't involve emotions.	−2 −1 0 +1 ⊕+2	15
	A good father.	Try to affirm what is good.	Mixed feelings of admiration and concern.	Removes the kids for long periods to do what he wants. 'Family' to him means his parents, siblings and our kids – not me.	−2 ⊖−1 0 +1 +2	6

Table 6.1 (continued)

a Positive aspects of the relationship

Question	Positives	Your response	Your feelings	Comment	Impact on you −2 = bad +2 = good	Ranking (both tables) 1 to 18
	Good at making money.	Try to raise ethical concerns.	Admire his success. Worried about his lack of business ethics.	Treats me like a customer to take advantage of.	−2 −1 0 +1 +2	7
	Wacky sense of humour and clever with words.	Smile.	Happy.	Affirms me. Doesn't happen much now.	−2 −1 0 +1 +2	14
2 What do you think your partner finds appealing about you?	Good looking and sexy.	Mixed reactions of pleasure and annoyance.	Mixed feelings – pride and shame.	Now treats this as an asset for his own status.	−2 −1 0 +1 +2	16

				Score	
Good mother.	Accept this.	Feel used.	He wanted good eggs and an incubator – not all of me. Would have divorced me if I hadn't produced kids.	⊖−2 −1 0 +1 +2	8
3 What is good about the way you interact with each other and with others?	Enjoy the company of other couples.	Relaxed and happy.	Pleasure in friendship and self-expression.	Can bounce ideas off others that I can't raise with him alone for fear of criticism.	−2 −1 ⓪ +1 +2	12
	Enjoy outings.	Make the most of them.	Excitement.	Not frequent as he says they're not cost-effective.	−2 −1 ⓪ +1 +2	17
	Both love our dog.	Respond with unrestrained affection.	Enjoyment and unconditional love.	We each give affection to the dog that we can't give each other.	−2 −1 0 +1 ⊕2	18

Score for positive aspects of the relationship =   +2

Table 6.1 (continued)

b Negative aspects of the relationship

Question	Negatives	Your response	Your feelings	Comment	Impact on you -2 = bad +2 = good	Ranking (both tables) 1 to 18
1 What do you find unappealing about your partner?	Sex repellent.	Try to avoid physical contact.	Disgust when we have sex, which is rarely – fortunately!	It wasn't like this at the beginning, I wonder whether it's because I now see him with open eyes.	-2 -1 0 +1 +2	3
	He has to set the agenda for everything.	I used to try to have a say, not anymore.	Feel my wishes don't matter. I don't exist.	He walks away or tells me I'm talking crap when I try to reason.	-2 -1 0 +1 +2	1
	He doesn't like my female friends – thinks they're troublemakers and too feminist.	I try to point to how they aren't like that.	Lonely because we used to share ideas but now he doesn't want to know.	Accuses me of motives I don't have, e.g. ball-breaking or hating his guts.	-2 - 0 +1 +2	13

2 What do you think your partner finds unappealing about you?					
Arguing back. It's OK when he does it: that's logic and debating.	I try to avoid making any contentious comments.	Defiant and unhappy as I feel unjustly criticized and blamed for creating marital strife when I express myself.	He goes away in a huff for several days after a disagreement. I think he has a girlfriend whose shoulder he can cry on.	(−2) –1 0 +1 +2	2
My Christian devotion and moral beliefs.	I make a stand on key Christian principles.	Angry – he says my faith and ethics are nonsense.	At the beginning he played along with what I believed in order to get me.	(−2) –1 0 +1 +2	4
Giving money to charity and those in need.	I give money, despite what he says as this is what Christians need to do.	Confused and upset.	He treats our money as if it's his and the needy are undeserving.	−2 (–1) 0 +1 +2	5

Table 6.1 (continued)

b Negative aspects of the relationship

Question	Negatives	Your response	Your feelings	Comment	Impact on you -2 = bad $+2$ = good	Ranking (both tables) 1 to 18
3 What is bad about the way you interact with each other and with others?	Lots of dismissive comments.	At first I took these in my stride, now I fight back.	Ashamed of myself for fighting dirty – angry with him for the same.	Self-protecting and self-defeating as the comments destroy the relationship.	⊘-2 -1 0 $+1$ $+2$	5
	Pretending our relationship is OK.	Try not to say anything that would upset him.	Feel hypocritical about the sham.	The easiest option for self-protection and avoiding conflict.	-2 ⊘-1 0 $+1$ $+2$	10
	Rejecting each other's home cooking.	I tried to cook what he liked, but now I cook what is easiest.	Alternately sad and powerful.	More about control than actual dietary preferences.	-2 ⊘-1 0 $+1$ $+2$	11

Score for negative aspects of the relationship = -15

Total score for positive and negative aspects = $+2 -15 = -12$

you've written and make any changes that reflect how you now think.

Whatever changes you make, ask yourself 'Why?' and 'What has happened since I last reviewed my answers to make me want to make this change?' When you make a change, explain the reason as this can give insight into your motives and feelings about the future.

Scoring

After the review period, add up the total score in the 'Impact on you' column in both tables. Subtract the minus score from the plus score. This is your total. The maximum scores are −32, if you had −2 for every point, or +32, if you had scored each point +2. In the hypothetical case of Jenny, the plusses in both tables below add up to +7 and the minuses come to −19. When the minuses are subtracted from the plusses, the total score is + 7 −19 = −12.

How reliable?

One important check on your reliability is how often you changed your mind when you reviewed your answers over the two months. The results are more reliable if changes are minor rather than a major rethink.

If you made major changes, the points you raised were what you were thinking at the time you wrote them, but you're still unsure. It's worth asking God for greater clarity and going back to your tables to continue recording your points honestly over the next few months until there's a relatively consistent pattern from weekly entries over a month.

How valid?

Those who know you and your spouse may not come to these conclusions, which raises the question of how to verify the validity of your answers. Maybe you find it hard to face the truth. Perhaps you've already made up your mind and are rationalizing your decision. Or possibly you're uncertain about wanting to make a decision and have avoided raising important issues.

Someone who knows you well could be helpful in confirming what you've written, suggesting other points you've missed or challenging your assessments. He or she may also ask probing questions to help you understand some of your underlying motives and biases. Counsellors are trained at doing this, but a wise friend can also be effective.

Make any changes to your tables which you consider valid. But don't treat the tables as the definitive word or use them or the methods you've applied as a weapon against your partner.

What do your results mean?

Although this is not a scientific test, the total score shows whether you believe your partnership is a good one or not. The scores and notes in Table 6.2 are based on how others responded and the way they rated their marriages.

As with many questionnaires, especially a subjective one like this, the greatest benefit comes from filling out the answers. It helps clarify what you really feel and believe about your marriage.

Jenny's answers

With Jenny's sample answers, the total score for both tables is −12. Jenny views the relationship with her husband as poor. Of special interest are the −1 and −2 scores for the positive aspects. For example, she notes as a positive that her partner thought she was a 'good mother', yet her feelings about this were negative, so she scored it −2. She explains that she felt used by her husband because he wanted good eggs and an incubator and would have divorced her if she hadn't produced children.

All the answers ranked 1 through to 5 are in the 'Negative aspects of the relationship' table. Each has a score of −2, giving a maximum total of −10 for the top five. In other words, Jenny considers the relationship is in serious trouble in the areas that really matter to her. The positive aspects Jenny rates as +2 were 'good to talk to', 'wacky sense of humour' and 'both love our dog', which are of low significance.

Table 6.2 Relationship assessment scores

Total scores	
+10 or higher	A moderate to high positive score suggests that you consider your partnership is good to very good. It raises the question of why you'd want to think of leaving. There may be one or two very significant negative factors making the relationship difficult. Nevertheless, the score would suggest the relationship has much going for it.
+9 to −9	There's a mixture of positive and negative. It will depend very much on which points you ranked at the top of the list as to whether you think there's hope.
−10 or lower	You regard your relationship as poor to very bad. A high negative score would indicate that you consider there are few redeeming qualities. Even some of the positive aspects may have negative overtones for you, which could make it difficult to continue in the relationship without major changes.
Scores of top five ranked items	Not all answers are of equal importance. The way you rank them shows what you believe is vital to the health of your relationship. Look at the first five most highly ranked points and total these scores.
+5 or higher	Unless there are one or two very serious flaws in the relationship, this would suggest you look again at why you're thinking of leaving.
−3 to +4	You consider the relationship is lacking in several vital areas, but not in others. Maybe the relationship has a chance, but it will probably require work.
−4 or lower	You firmly believe that the relationship is poor in the areas you regard as critical. It will take a lot of work to turn the situation around.

Checking your assessment against the criteria for marriage breakdown

A high negative score shows that you believe there are things wrong with your relationship. It suggests that the relationship has broken down. There is even more chance of this if you also got a high score on the Relationship self-check in Chapter 3, pp. 33–5. That doesn't mean, though, that your relationship is beyond repair. You could have focused on issues at the periphery of your marriage. For example, you might have high negative scores because of poor communication, yet fail to mention you're intimate in other ways.

Does your assessment fit one or more of the six criteria for a marriage breakdown described in the previous chapter? As a reminder, these are:

1 There's failure to meet your essential emotional needs.
2 There's a critical lack of commitment.
3 There's a serious lack of trust.
4 You and your partner have major value differences.
5 The relationship is very unfair.
6 There's serious abuse.

Check out your top five ranked items against these criteria to see which ones, if any, apply.

Jenny's top five ranked points include comments like, 'He has to set the agenda for everything', 'Feel my wishes don't matter. I don't exist'. 'Feel I can't express myself', 'Unjustly criticized', 'He says my faith and ethics are nonsense' and 'Sex repellent', which were all scored negatively. Her remarks imply there's a breakdown of communication, power plays, anger and other negative feelings. Is this sufficient to show something's wrong at the heart of the marriage?

Some of Jenny's remarks apply to the above criteria more than others. Regarding sex with her partner as a 'repellent' and expressing personal feelings of loneliness suggest that the relationship fails to meet Jenny's emotional needs. Jenny's most common complaint is that she considers the relationship unfair and unequal because she feels her husband has to set the agenda, he criticizes her unfairly if she argues back, she felt used as an 'incubator' and now feels used as a mother, his family takes priority over her, he treats her like a customer and their money as if it's his.

'He says my faith and ethics are nonsense' and attitudes over giving money to charity and those in need imply major differences in values. Comments about a girlfriend and how family means his parents, siblings and the kids rather than her, suggest her husband demonstrates serious lack of commitment.

Jenny's comments, ratings and scores point to marriage breakdown. The reasons come out as incredibly unfair and unequal treatment, major value differences, essential emotional needs not being met and lack of commitment.

To take this hypothetical example to a conclusion that satisfies Jenny as a Christian, we see her giving her responses much thought over the next few years and talking about them with clergy, church friends and relatives. She is persistent in asking God to help her with her marriage and to make the problems and the answer clear to her. After trying hard to make the marriage work through forgiveness, caring, kindness, perseverance and marriage counselling, she feels her efforts are in vain and God wants her to separate from her husband. Several years after they begin living apart, her husband asks for a divorce so he can marry again. Jenny is pleased he has found someone more suitable, and seven years after leaving her husband, Jenny marries a man with whom she feels compatible, including sharing similar Christian beliefs and practices.

Although Jenny eventually leaves her husband, she clearly tries through the grace of God to do all she can to stay in the relationship.

Jenny's example leads us into the second principle (see p. 53): genuine attempts have been made to save the marriage and bring about a workable reconciliation.

7

Saving your marriage

---•◦•---

First steps to recovery

Your marriage may have broken down, but don't write it off until you've made a genuine effort to save it. There are plenty of couples who pull back from the brink of divorce to live happy lives together. Of course, if one of you has changed sexual orientation or your partner is engaged to be married to someone else, it'll come down to how you say goodbye. But if there's a glimmer of hope, it's worth pursing. And the sooner you start the better.

It has to be a genuine effort though, as your spouse will detect whether you're half-hearted.

Begin by asking God to help and guide you and your partner to do what is best for your relationship. Take to heart what Jesus said, 'Come to me, all you who are weary and burdened, and I will give you rest' (Matt. 11.28). He also said, 'Whatever you ask for in prayer, believe that you have received it, and it will be yours' (Mark 11.24). Whenever you feel frustrated, upset or overwhelmed, take time out to offer all your worries to God and then spend time quietly in his presence absorbing his love and strength. That doesn't mean it will be easy for you or you'll get the answers you want. Instead, you're acknowledging that God is with you and that what he wants matters most.

It's harder to bring about reconciliation if one of you has moved out of your home. So, unless you need to leave to protect yourself or your family from your partner, it's worth staying together until you're sure the marriage is irretrievable.

Let your spouse know that you love him or her, and that you're committed to your relationship and prepared to fight to save it. And mean it by putting aside any hurt or anger you feel about the relationship and listening – without interruption – to what your spouse has to say. Try to understand what he or she is really feeling. Listen for neglected needs like intimacy, affection and romance, or for complaints about your bad habits.

Respect your partner's views and feelings, even when they're strongly stated, whether you agree or disagree with them. Strong emotions are involved in intimate relationships and they need to be treated as important, not brushed aside by telling your partner to stop being so emotional and to concentrate on rational solutions. Casting blame, bearing a grudge, trying to defend yourself or offering your own solution to problems will sabotage efforts at reconciliation. If you're serious, saying, 'Yes, dear', and doing what your spouse wants is the best response at this point.

The final straw came when Rob complained that his wife, Marilyn, had served him pasta and rice dishes for four weeks in a row. He said he longed for steak and chips. Marilyn retorted that she was doing two jobs – her day job and most of the housework – whereas Rob came home from work and watched TV. She said her only consolation under the circumstances was to cook what she wanted.

Rob reckoned he had a more demanding career, and he did his bit by putting out the garbage, arranging car repairs, paying the bills and doing the cooking at barbeques and on the few occasions when Marilyn was sick or late home from work. He laughingly pointed to how he was an awful cook and how women cooked in most families, although the best chefs in the world were men. This added insult to injury as far as Marilyn was concerned.

Marilyn became increasingly unhappy while Rob side-stepped further conflicts by joining his friends at the pub. When offered a promotion to a job in another town, Marilyn seized the opportunity: 'I've had being your slave. We've grown apart and there's not much use in staying together.'

This time Rob was genuinely shocked. His first instinct was to respond as he had always done by defending himself and pointing to how irrational Marilyn was being. But he quickly grasped that this was the last thing he should say as it would reinforce Marilyn in her decision to leave. Instead, he said, 'I love you very much', did everything she wanted and made a point of listening to what had happened during her day. He cooked the evening meal for the rest of the week and did a good deal of the housework. He even enrolled in a cooking class.

Marilyn doubted whether this dramatic turnaround would last. But it did. Rob resigned from his job and uprooted to the new town to support Marilyn's career advancement. Slowly their relationship improved and they agreed to a roster for housework. They even divided the cooking between them and once a week they prepared a meal together, which gave them a chance to catch up with the details of each other's life. Rob's reaction was not what Marilyn expected. Yet it was what she wanted.

There's a difference between doing what your partner wants and submission. Rob wasn't a doormat: he was addressing the core problem, which was for a fairer relationship over simple daily household routines.

What if your spouse uses the threat to leave as a means of getting his or her own way? Marilyn now knows all she needs to do to get Rob to comply with her wishes is to say, 'I'm leaving you.' Christians who are married to non-Christians sometimes complain of how their spouses use their Christianity against them with comments like, 'I thought you Christians are meant to go the extra mile', or 'Aren't you meant to be more forgiving?'

Listening to your partner's needs and trying to meet what is reasonable is not the same as giving in to emotional blackmail. A partner whose demands are unreasonable or who constantly threatens to leave is being unfair. It may be helpful to establish clear expectations and boundaries (see 'Boundaries' below, p. 100).

It's far more effective to change behaviour and attitudes through positive rather than negative reinforcement. We'd rather be affirmed than censured. This was the principle Rob used to good effect to reverse Marilyn's negative attitude to their marriage. He affirmed how important Marilyn was to him and gradually her response affirmed him in the changes he was making.

Aim to remove whatever is coming between you. It could be a matter of switching off the TV and going to bed earlier, resigning from an organization that is taking up too much of your leisure time or seeking a less demanding job.

If your partner accuses you of nagging, bite your tongue when you're tempted to nag again, say nothing and then affirm your partner when he or she does something that pleases you. If you've nagged your partner to pick his or her dirty laundry off the bedroom floor in the past, then perhaps praise wouldn't go amiss for helping with the laundry or vacuum-cleaning the bedroom. This carries the added bonus of turning your attention away from what you don't like to what you do like about your partner.

Similarly, if your partner complains that you don't listen to him or her, consciously set aside times to listen rather than give your views. You may feel you already know what's on your spouse's mind, but often he or she just wants to know you listen and care.

Don't try to change everything at once or make promises that you know you can't keep, like insisting, 'I'll change.' Your partner has probably heard that one before. Unless you have specific and realistic goals, trying to overcome a bad habit within a week is like going on a crash diet. It will only lead to disappointment and deepen the lack of trust. Similarly, don't expect your partner to meet all your needs or to change his or her basic personality for you. This is a recipe for disappointment.

Follow Rob's example by beginning with several realistic and easy to achieve objectives. Once you've met these, add others so that you gradually reshape your behaviour and attitudes towards your spouse and your relationship. You may find that a counsellor or a good friend can advise and support you while you try to make these changes.

If you find your spouse ignores or is irritated by your efforts no matter what you do to change your behaviour, this could suggest that he or she has already decided to leave you. Whatever you do will only help confirm that decision (see Chapter 3, p. 24). You may need to recognize after several weeks of trying for reconciliation that little you do at this stage will make a difference.

Riding out the storm

In the same way that we need time to recover from an illness, sometimes the best way to save a marriage is to be prayerful, patient and supportive, and allow time for healing.

John's case is mentioned in Chapter 3, pp. 26–7. He was laid off from work and felt dispirited, drank heavily, neglected his appearance and vented his negative feelings on his wife, Ruth. When he finally got the kind of job he was looking for, the change in him was remarkable. He gave up his bad habits and was very appreciative of Ruth's sticking by him. He admitted he'd been unbearable: 'To think I nearly drove you out of my life because I couldn't cope with being out of work. Yet you stood by me and I love you for it.' Their relationship grew because of the experience.

Linda Waite and her team (see p. 75) found that about four out of five of those who were unhappy with their marriages at a particular point turned out to be happy five years later. Some of these were couples who rode out 'Crisis discontent' (see p. 24). Their marriages had been hit by a major crisis that had upset their relationship, but by stubbornly staying together and riding out the storm they found that the crisis had eventually passed or been resolved.

Recognize that it could take time for the situation to change. But if your relationship doesn't improve when everyone else perceives the crisis is over or a reasonable time for healing has passed, then you may need to seek help from others. Alternatively, you may have to warn your partner that you can't put up with the situation much longer and you want to work together at finding a good solution.

Counselling

In spite of the prevalence of marriage counselling services and the effectiveness of most therapy styles, the majority of partners whose marriages are in difficulty do not seek counselling. Those couples who do seek counselling often come to it too late, have unrealistic expectations or stop too soon. One or both of the partners may not want to change or be unable to change their behaviour.

As wives are more likely to initiate a break, men and women may have different agendas for using counsellors. Contrary to popular belief, husbands do seek marriage counselling – usually after their wives say they want to leave – even though men feel counsellors will automatically assume they're guilty of causing the marriage breakdown. Linda Waite and her team found that husbands tend to choose counsellors who want the marriage to succeed and who are genuinely interested in their clients.

Counselling can be for individuals, couples, families or groups of people. Counsellors have different training and styles. Some encourage introspection and delve into motives and experiences that shape your behaviour. Others concentrate on activities that will modify attitudes and behaviour. Many use a mixture of approaches depending on your needs.

Counsellors may be in private practice or operate out of non-profit organizations, including churches, or through Relationship Services (Relate). Government agencies may also offer counselling services. Usually, counsellors are registered or belong to a professional organization and agree to operate according to ethical codes of conduct. Clergy operate under church codes of conduct.

The type of counselling you seek and the person you choose as a counsellor will depend on the issues bothering you. Ask around, check with counselling and therapy associations (usually listed in telephone directories and on the internet) and with potential counsellors. Find out how each operates and any costs involved before committing yourself. If after a session or two, you find your counsellor's style is unsuitable, seek another counsellor.

Generally, counselling gives an opportunity to raise important matters privately and in confidence. The counsellor encourages you to reflect on what you've raised and to sort through feelings, issues and priorities. You receive help to act on your new insights, put your problems into perspective and face tricky decisions and future challenges with fresh confidence.

It's important you let your counsellor know what you want from the counselling: whether you want to save your marriage, check that you're doing the right thing in deciding to leave or want help in leaving. You may need to think of separate counselling as individuals to begin with if you and your partner have very different agendas. Also, if you're uncertain as to whether to leave or stay in your marriage and don't want to alarm your partner unnecessarily, you may need individual counselling before seeking couples' counselling.

Counselling for couples and families is different from counselling for individuals and requires special training. Joint counselling is usually more successful at saving marriages than individual counselling because couples continue to interact and have the opportunity to discuss and encourage changes between sessions. But it requires both of you being keen to benefit from the counselling rather than trying to compete with each other to prove your side of the story to the counsellor.

Avoid joint counselling if abuse is involved. Joint counselling implies there's a 50/50 partnership problem, which is not the case in an abusive relationship. Even if the abuse is provoked, the abuser needs to take full responsibility for the behaviour, which he or she is usually reluctant to learn how to do. The abuser may also be angered by what happens during the counselling session and take it out on a spouse when they get home.

Counsellors see you only about an hour a week, whereas you have an ongoing relationship with friends who are involved in your everyday life. Linda Waite's research team discovered that when husbands behaved badly, it was the influence of others, especially their male friends, putting pressure on them to reform that had the greatest impact.

But you may need to confer with your spouse before inviting others to contribute their support and prayers as it could be hurtful to him or her to learn you've told others about your private life. It could also raise questions of confidentiality, bias and conflict of loyalty for your friends, who may be just as close to your partner.

Working on it together

Perhaps you've grown apart because of different interests, work schedules and demands, or just sheer exhaustion. There's little intimacy and emotional support any more. You're living together but your former soulmate is now your cellmate and you know that once you lead with the ominous words, 'We need to talk', you will open a can of worms.

One way out of the impasse is to suggest something less subjective or threatening, such as the Relationship self-check in Chapter 3, pp. 33–5, followed by comparing results and discussing what you both need to do next. That's if your partner agrees.

You may find that your partner is surprised at your negative assessment in the Relationship self-check. He or she may have no idea you feel this way and be relieved a meaningful dialogue can now take place to improve the relationship. It could also go the other way and fail to reveal anything helpful.

Following the Relationship self-check, it could be useful for you both also to complete the Relationship assessment in Chapter 6, pp. 76–89, and compare your responses. You may then find it worthwhile to prepare a plan for what you might do to improve the relationship as shown in the Relationship issues table (Table 7.1). It may seem too clinical and businesslike for dealing with the emotional complexity and subtleties of marriage, but it could be an effective way forward.

Relationship issues table

Draw up a Relationship issues table as shown in Table 7.1. This will help formulate what you both want, help you come to decisions and provide a record of what you've decided and how your decisions will be implemented, along with any other relevant comments which will avoid confusion and misunderstandings.

Begin by each of you listing the issues that are important to you. Take turns writing them down. Stick to a few key issues where a change will really make a difference. In a separate column state what each of you thinks the solution should be, then compare your views and seek a solution. Where there are differences, look to ways to reach a compromise or a trade-off.

Record your solution, how to implement the solution, whom it applies to and when it will be implemented. Under 'Comments', note

Table 7.1 Relationship issues table

Issue	Jim's view	Mary's view	Solution	How	Who	When	Comments
TV sport.	It's my only pleasure in life.	It comes between me and Jim.	Jim and Mary accommodate each other.	Both to make their TV watching more intentional.	Jim becomes more selective in his TV watching/ Mary watches with him from time to time.	When work round the house is done (unless there's a really important game on!)	Watching sport on TV is something to look forward to for both.
Sex infrequent and boring.	Need to do something to spice it up, but Mary's not interested.	Jim treats sex as separate from intimacy.	Need to spend more time being intimate before sex.	Schedule time for intimacy.	Both.	Agree on time twice a week.	Intimacy is necessary before Mary can respond to Jim's desires.

A special holiday.	Can't afford it.	Do it while we can, even if it means going without other things.	Both agree on a ceiling price.	Make a list of what we want from a holiday. Reduce to five main points.	Both.	Don't rush it.	Jim accepts the need for a second honeymoon. Mary realizes a modest holiday might be as much fun.
Don't have much in common any more.	I would like to do more things together, like movies, restaurants.	We need to chat more and do things together like gardening.	Accommodate each other.	Allow time for discussion over meals. Go to movies together and both do gardening.	Take turns to cook and select movies.	Discussion once a day and a joint activity once a week.	Jim is keen to date Mary and woo her. Mary wants more contact.

any issues, provisos, questions or other thoughts that are pertinent to your solution, such as trade-offs like, 'I'll help more with housework, if you'll go to bed earlier with me.'

In Table 7.1 are four issues, two from each spouse. The solutions and what needs to be done to implement each solution are for a hypothetical couple, Jim and Mary, who are in a typical state of creeping discontent. Not so typical is that they are both unhappy and prepared to address this together early in the process. The rows with the white background are Mary's issues while those with the grey background are the issues Jim raised.

The responses suggest that Jim and Mary aren't relating as a loving couple. They feel they are moving apart and need to do something about this. The strategies they suggest are positive ones that accommodate preferences and differences.

Boundaries

Expectations and boundaries usually emerge in early stages of relationships. We know when not to interrupt our partner, when we annoy and when we please him or her. But sometimes boundaries become blurred or are not obvious. You may need to clarify what you expect from each other, especially where a partner might have second thoughts about expectations such as having children; or where there's abuse, neglect, an extra-marital affair; or if your partner wants to dominate you or take an unfair advantage.

The boundaries and what happens when they're crossed would vary depending on the circumstances. If you've agreed to zero tolerance to physical violence, you're both accepting that either of you could leave if one of you threatens the family's safety. In other cases, you might decide that the first time your partner crosses the line, you respond with a warning. If it happens again, you give a second warning. The third warning is the final one. After that, your partner must seek help. If that fails, then you will consider separation.

The downside is that it can make your partner feel you're treating the marriage like an employment contract – stating performance criteria and what happens when someone doesn't make the grade.

Your spouse might agree to your boundaries in theory, but in practice he or she may react by feeling you're not allowing enough room for mistakes and forgiveness.

It's important to forgive, but forgiveness shouldn't be used as a licence to repeat bad behaviour. In forgiving someone, you expect repentance and determination through the grace of God to change for the better. You may not want to act like a boss who fires staff because of poor performance, but you should expect a genuine effort to improve.

Time out

Is it worth you both taking time out from your marriage while you clear the air and sort out how you feel about each other? After all, doesn't absence make the heart grow fonder? This does work sometimes, but not if either of you is seriously thinking of leaving.

In her book, *The Marriage Sabbatical: The Journey That Brings You Home*, Cheryl Jarvis argues, after interviewing 55 middle-aged married women, that a personal sabbatical or time out from daily routines for several weeks or months can be a positive experience. The time out is for 'creative, professional, or spiritual growth, for study, reflection or renewal'. It enables individual growth and a special dream to be pursued. Like any sabbatical, it's planned for a positive purpose. She doesn't suggest this as an emotional escape or disguised separation. You might also consider taking a retreat at a monastery or other retreat house, to read, reflect and pray about your marriage.

Nevertheless, if your relationship is in trouble, unless your partner went on a similar retreat, he or she may construe any time out as a trial separation or a prelude to ending the relationship. The separation may also reinforce the advantages of living apart and make reconciliation more difficult.

Marriage groups and programmes

Marriage groups are usually support teams where couples learn from one another and examine what's good about their relationships, as well as look at ways of coping with problems. Members of some marriage groups have problems in common, like an addiction, but most groups usually have more general membership.

Marriage courses and programmes typically have a set theme or goal and are for a specific time, such as a weekend retreat or a block of sessions. While having the same aims as marriage groups, they are more tightly controlled around an agenda. Often these groups divide into male and female sub-groups so that each can explore their expectations and how they react in relationships. They then look at these together and may practise exercises in meeting needs of intimacy and communication.

Many churches support Christian marriage enrichment (ME) programmes that aim to improve communication between married couples, help them overcome problems together and experience more fully the biblical basis of marriage. Specially trained counsellors work with couples to identify the strengths, growth and dysfunctional aspects of the relationship. A weekend retreat with other couples is usually involved.

The advantage of group work is recognizing you have issues in common with other couples, often leading to mutual and ongoing encouragement and support.

A possible disadvantage would be ending up in a group which doesn't understand your issues. One woman told me how she was the only one wanting to leave her partner in a group of ex-married people who'd been left by their spouse. She had to bear the brunt of their pain. So, check first what kind of group it is.

Another obvious disadvantage is exposing yourself and your marriage to others. You or your partner may disclose something the other considers private, which could damage trust. To avoid this problem, set parameters as to what you can and can't reveal.

A drawback to short-term programmes is that they can have the same effect as many motivational courses: you may feel inspired during the course and maybe for a week or two afterwards, but unless there's constant reinforcement you soon revert to old ways. Much depends on the follow-up support and encouragement. Studies of

ME programmes found they had limited effectiveness without this follow up support.

If you or your spouse has a serious behaviour problem that's ruining the marriage (and maybe other relationships as well), such as emotional or physical abuse, alcohol or drug dependence or a gambling addiction, then groups dealing with anger management, Alcoholics Anonymous, Gamblers Anonymous, and so on, may be the best solution. These groups have the advantage of being able to focus on the particular problem and how it affects loved ones. They also offer support and encouragement from others who've had similar experiences. Such groups are easy to find in a telephone directory and on the internet.

If over the next few months the situation gets no better, ask God if there's anything else you can do. Remain open for the Holy Spirit to work through others, like your counsellor, clergy, others in your Christian community or friends. If that doesn't work, accept that the relationship has broken down and can't reasonably be salvaged. For a Christian, that means that prayer, perseverance, forgiveness and seeking God's love are unable to heal the rift.

The situation might change for the better at some future date, but at this stage you've done all that anyone can reasonably expect of you.

8

Stay or leave? The issues

————•◆•————

In pursuit of happiness

You might be unhappy in your marriage, but how do you know whether you, your spouse and your children (if you have any) will be better off if you split? Does it matter if you break your partner's heart? Would God really want you to leave, and how do you decide whether you've met the third key principle (p. 54)? This says: the split gives you and others who are affected a better chance of long-term happiness than if you stayed together. For a Christian that implies that the kingdom of God and his will are better fulfilled by you leaving your partner.

This raises the question of whether, as Christians, we should be seeking happiness. Jesus certainly didn't seek personal happiness through his relationships with others, and neither did the Apostles. Their focus was on being faithful to God. Shouldn't we be trying to be faithful to God and our partner by staying in our marriage?

Yes, we should try to be faithful to God and our spouse, but not if our marriage is going to be a pointless lifetime sentence of misery and unhappiness which no longer fulfils the purposes for which God ordained it.

Whether partners are in fact happier leaving is a research topic with inconsistent findings.

Studies like that of Linda Waite and her team (p. 75) found the vast majority of unhappy couples who stayed in their marriages reported they were happy five years later. They also found that a second marriage didn't guarantee happiness. Those who remarried were generally no happier than those who stayed with their original partner.

Judith Wallerstein came to a different conclusion. From following what happened to 60 middle class Californian families coping with divorce, she learned that many ex-partners, especially women, grow in competence and self-esteem. Many second marriages are happier than the first. On the downside, she found that not all recover from the split. Some ex-partners remain angry, hurt or humiliated for many years. Younger men may have difficulty developing as husbands and fathers in new relationships. Many women with young children face poverty and find it difficult to cope. Older people have fewer opportunities to make a new life.

From her extensive studies of divorced people, University of Virginia psychology professor emeritus E. Mavis Hetherington concluded that while the break-up can be painful and disruptive for the first few years, 'divorce is a reasonable solution to an unhappy, acrimonious, destructive marital relationship. It can be a gateway to pathways associated with joy, satisfaction, and attainments, not just with loss, pain, and failure.'

Different aims and research methods, including measures of happiness, may account for some of the differences. Funding for family research often comes from those who are keen to foster stable families, which can alter the focus. Maybe the only conclusion from these conflicting results is that whether you choose to stay or leave, time can heal.

While research results give insights, they may not help you predict what will bring greater happiness to you and your family. In a way, it's similar to deciding whether to marry. You're trying to envisage what it will be like in the future based on existing feelings, insights and information.

Will splitting solve your problems?

Leaving your spouse is different from ending a teenage romance. As a married couple, you're physically, emotionally, spiritually and materially bound together. For years, you've invested a huge part of yourself in the relationship. You may also have children and other important people who depend on you. So, a split will be a psychological amputation that will raise plenty of issues and lots of emotion.

If someone you loved has died, you'll have some idea of how you respond emotionally to loss. But there's a difference. Your partner will survive after you break up and how he or she behaves will continue to affect you.

There are the obvious practical questions. How do you divide assets and responsibilities, including the rearing and financial costs of children, if you have any?

Do you need legal or financial advisors? Where will you live?

Going solo may include changes in daily routines, a drop in income and standard of living, relocation to a different home, solo parenting or less access to your children, coping with your kids' reactions to your divorce, new employment, loss of friends, lack of intimacy and loneliness. Unless you're on a good income, you'll probably spend more time and energy meeting basic needs than you did before.

How the break affects your dependants may also concern you greatly, leading you to shower affection on your children – and then worry about whether you're over-compensating or acting in a dysfunctional way.

Some people and organizations may attempt to take advantage of your vulnerability. Lawyers and financial advisors might prolong processes or suggest strategies more to their financial advantage than your interests.

Recently separated younger women regularly complain of how men target them in the belief that they will be an easy conquest. It can happen to men too.

Although you'll be wary of emotional attachments, you'll still have emotional needs. There'll be a temptation to rush into an unsuitable relationship or to have casual sex out of desperation.

'I would do anything to have a warm body beside me again', was how one man who had been divorced for nine months expressed how he and many in his position feel. Several one-night stands left him feeling he had used others and been used for selfish reasons, leaving him emotionally unfulfilled and nostalgic for the intimacy he once had with his wife. His reaction is typical. Researchers have found casual sex after a break-up can often have the opposite effect from the one desired, especially on women who may feel lonely, unloved, unhappy, and suffer low self-respect.

You may blame yourself and feel guilty for your marriage break-up. You will probably feel wary of future relationships, and even more so if it's your second or third marriage breakdown.

Although many do find greater happiness the second time they marry, the number of divorced people whose next marriage also ends in divorce raises the question whether splitting will really solve anything.

To reduce the risk of repeating relationship mistakes or creating new problems that deprive you, and others, of happiness, you'll need to make a thorough and realistic assessment of the issues you're likely to face and how you'll cope with these challenges. You may decide the split will create more problems than it will solve. Or you may conclude that after the break-up there will be a trade-off of initial problems associated with leaving for potential long-term happiness. The assessment in Chapter 9, pp. 117–28, may help with this process.

Your health

The stresses and strains of an unhappy marriage can affect your physical and mental health. Your partner and kids may be suffering too. So it's natural to assume you'll feel a whole lot better once you escape the cause of the tension.

But, despite a popular belief that becoming single again will reduce the stresses and strains experienced in married life, it can do the opposite. Statistically, divorce is more harmful to your health than smoking more than a pack a day.

Deborah suffered from a stress-related illness when she was with her abusive husband, Andy, mentioned in Chapter 5, pp. 73–4. When she finally left him, she felt relief to begin with. But that didn't last:

Leaving proved more stressful than I thought it would be. The parishioners were supportive, which helped. But going out alone when you've been married isn't easy. I felt emotionally and physically drained. I must've caught every flu virus around. I spent a fortune on doctor's bills. I used to have a perfect driving record, yet I kept on having minor road accidents. That ruined my insurance no claims bonus.

As Deborah discovered, separation is a traumatic experience that can lower the body's immune system. This ups your chances of illness, infection, heart disease and cancer. Compared with being married, separation and divorce may make you lonelier, prone to accidents and injury, susceptible to substance abuse, depression, schizophrenia, anxiety-related disorders, self-inflicted wounds, and early death from disease or suicide.

In 1967, Thomas Holmes and Richard Rahe developed their very popular simple stress test known as the Social Readjustment Rating Scale. This assumes there's a strong relationship between the stress that comes with change in our lives and illness and accidents. They included in their test over 40 of the typical stresses we might face, giving each a score. Rated highest is the death of a spouse, followed by divorce and then separation. At the lower end of the scale is a minor violation of the law. The higher your total stress score the greater your chances of illness or injury.

Although divorce is near the top of the list, it produces only a 20 per cent chance of new health problems. Yet, there's more to divorce than cutting your ex out of your wedding photos and your will. The test also measures changes in financial circumstances, living standard, social situation, working conditions, personal habits and so on. It's when separation and divorce are associated with added stresses like these – as they nearly always are – that the score skyrockets into the high-risk zone. This creates around an 80 per cent chance of ill health or accident until you readjust to the changes.

The divorce health statistics make grim reading and are frequently quoted by pro-marriage and conservative divorce-reform advocates.

Few scholars compare the health and death rates of the happily married with the unhappily married. Nor does the basic stress test of Holmes and Rahe measure many of the stresses involved when a marriage is in difficulty.

What research there is on unhappy couples confirms what most of us know from experience. Stress usually begins well before couples split. Symptoms may include anger, depression, substance abuse, stress-related illnesses and poorer work performance. Unhappy spouses tend to be less happy about life in general. They also have lower levels of personal mastery and self-worth than those who are happily married. In other words, staying in an ailing relationship where we're not able to have regular close emotional support can also be bad for our health.

Whether you decide to stay or leave your marriage, look to ways you can reduce the stress and protect your health. This may include planning practical strategies to cope with changes so that there are few surprises; giving high priority to healthy food, regular sleep, relaxation, recreation and exercise routines, close friendships and regular social activity; seeking early help from friends and health professionals when you're not coping well.

Your partner's happiness

Are you responsible for your partner's happiness?

'Even though our marriage isn't working, he still loves me. I don't want to hurt him. Yet, if I don't leave, I'll be miserable living a lie. What shall I do?' This could be your dilemma.

'Look after you' is a common answer. 'It seems selfish, but it's for the best. If you worry about your partner and everyone else, you'll please nobody, least of all yourself.'

This comes across as reasonable but it has four basic flaws.

First, you won't find it quite so easy to ignore your spouse. You've shared an intimate relationship and unless you're emotionally numb or despise your spouse, you'll still have feelings of concern. As his or her happiness is affected by what you decide, if at all possible you're likely to want your partner to be happy too.

Second, ignoring your partner's happiness can have a negative impact on your own happiness, especially if he or she thinks you're selfish and unfair. Your spouse may want to get even and make life difficult for you. Your apparent self-centredness could also make a potential new partner wary.

Third, in time you may come to feel shame or guilt over how you ignored your spouse, especially if he or she suffers badly from your decision.

Fourth, as Christians we have a responsibility to treat everyone, even our enemies – and our spouse – with the same kind of love that Jesus showed to others.

What if your partner will seriously suffer from your leaving? Perhaps you'll break his or her heart and it will take a long time to heal, or may never heal. Maybe he or she has given up a career to care for you and the kids and now future work and earning prospects are limited.

If something like this is the case, you may still decide to leave the relationship but you will need to do it in a way that will reduce the negative impact on your partner. For instance, to help your spouse adjust to your decision, you might choose to stay in the relationship until a time when leaving is more beneficial to your partner, or both of you may go through a phased withdrawal (see Chapter 10, p. 132), seeking relationship exit counselling or guidance for job retraining and recruitment.

What if age, loss of looks or personal appeal means your partner is likely to spend the rest of his or her life lonely and unhappy? Perhaps he or she has a disability or illness and is dependent on you. Under these circumstances, leaving your marriage exacts a high toll from your partner. Is that fair?

One good test of what is fair is to think of how the community at large would react. Imagine your decision appearing in the national press? 'Christian husband leaves invalid wife and five kids for exotic dancer' or 'Wife dumps unemployed husband to start multi-million pound business'. While these are unlikely to be the headlines that apply to your situation, they do raise the question of what's reasonable.

The answer may vary depending on the circumstances of your partner. You may decide that 'for better or for worse' means that because of the greater unhappiness your partner is likely to experience compared to your own hopes for future happiness, you have a duty to stay even though the marriage has taken a turn for the worse as far as you're concerned. If you're financially well off, coming to a decision that involves continuing to provide care for a disabled partner may be an option. Again, a phased withdrawal that enables your partner to adjust may be the appropriate way to go.

Maybe you're fearful of what will happen if you leave. Perhaps your partner will become sick, depressed or suicidal, resort to alcohol, suffer an accident, perform poorly at work, lose his or her job or have to live on welfare and charity. Your spouse may even use emotional blackmail to try to force you to stay, knowing that you'll feel guilty and responsible for the problems.

But is the possibility of something negative happening to your partner sufficient reason for staying? After all, divorce does cause distress and there's always a risk of it having a negative impact on a partner's health and finances – as it could on your own.

Maybe it's simply a case of laying the groundwork to help your partner cope. Jesus reminds us of the Golden Rule, 'So in everything, do to others what you would have them do to you, for this sums up the Law and the Prophets' (Matt. 7.12). It's worth imagining what kind of treatment you would want for anyone else, including yourself, if they, or you, were in your partner's shoes.

Even though your fears for your partner may be well founded, don't be surprised if they don't materialize. The shock of Leonard's leaving, mentioned in Chapter 5, pp. 70–2, turned Joan around.

For the kids' sake

When you consider the enormous physical, psychological and emotional change that children experience when their parents split, is it any wonder that couples with young kids take a long time to decide whether to get a divorce?

Not only is the order and predictable pattern of life upset, but the kids' trust in their parents, whom they depend on for love and nurture as a couple, is broken. Even adult children who are in their twenties or thirties get angry and upset when their parents break up in their later years.

Generally, though, from 70 to 80 per cent of children adjust to the divorce of their parents and most believe in hindsight it was for the best. However, a few children do suffer behavioural problems, don't do as well as they might at school and have difficulty forming committed intimate relationships, especially in their early adult years. Nevertheless, these problems could have surfaced just as easily if the parents had stayed together in an unhappy relationship for the kids' sake.

At the time it's hard to see it's all for the best, especially when the disruption includes a drop in household income and standard of living, especially for kids who live with mothers, whose income is usually lower than that of the children's fathers. Relocation to a new address and changes in education and social standing all undermine confidence and contribute to feelings of loneliness. Your kids' academic performance may fall and their anxiety manifest in physical symptoms like headaches, stomach aches and disturbed sleep.

While dealing with their own grief, they'll also have to cope with yours. You may try to hide your hurt feelings to protect them, but hiding feelings is not the same as hiding birthday presents. They're your offspring, so they know you intimately and will quickly sense how you're really feeling. They are likely to feel powerless to help and may even believe they are to blame for the split.

If you're the parent who doesn't have custody (usually the father), you'll probably want to compensate by treating each visit as if it were the kids' birthday. If you're the other partner, you'll find it tempting to blame all behavioural problems on your ex's contradictory rules and routines.

Straddling the two worlds of separated parents is a balancing act for kids. They may cope by treating each world as separate and switch behaviour when they move between parents. If they take sides, it's usually because it's in their own interest.

If you feel overburdened, you may resort to a variety of caregivers or count on your kids to take over much of the housekeeping, expecting the older ones to baby-sit and help bring up their younger brothers and sisters. Loneliness may drive you to turn to an older child, especially a teenager, for emotional support and friendship. This alters the child-parent relationship by asking of children emotional maturity and understanding beyond their years.

The scene changes yet again when a new partner, a new job or some other activity comes along to bring new happiness to the parent. The kids are no longer the main focus of attention.

Your dating can be an emotional rollercoaster ride for you and the kids. They may like one of your dates more than you do or loathe someone you like. Jealousy is common and your children may try to sabotage your new love life.

If you do remarry or live with a partner (most divorced people do within a few years), your standard of living may improve to your kids' liking, but there could be new stresses. They'll have a new step-parent and probably stepbrothers and stepsisters, or face the arrival of a new baby from your union. The oldest in your previous marriage might now be one of the youngest in your new marriage. There may be resentment and conflict of values with your stepchildren, or conflict of loyalty between the kids' stepparents and their biological parents. It's hardly surprising that it can take many years for blended families to adjust. Nor is it surprising that the divorce rate among remarried couples with stepfamilies is considerably higher than that of others who marry again.

There has been massive research and debate on the effects of separation and divorce on children. Psychologist Judith Wallerstein concluded from her research that divorce is nearly always more devastating to children than adults. Only one in ten of the children she interviewed was relieved by the marriage break-up and that was because violence was involved. Most felt that when a parent left, they, too, were rejected. Wallerstein also found that 'one cannot predict the long-term effects of divorce on children from how they react at the outset'. Some of the most disturbed kids at the time of the split were fine 10 years later. Others who seemed to take it in their stride were having problems 10 and 15 years later. Most considered they had grown up under the shadow of their parents' divorce. Many had difficulty forming fulfilling, faithful and lasting relationships. Nearly half were anxious, underachieving, self-effacing and sometimes angry.

Recent research throws doubt on some of Judith Wallerstein's conclusions. The parental split may not be to blame for all the children's behavioural problems. And the legacy of divorce may not be so long term.

Yongmin Sun and Yuanzhang Li studied nearly 10,000 adolescents at four different times before and after their parents split. They found problems began to surface well before the divorce. According to Yongmin Sun,

> The damage in children's psychological well-being is already observable three years prior to divorce, but gets worse as the divorce approaches. Yet, as the event of divorce recedes, the detrimental effect becomes smaller, indicating a recovery in children's psychological well-being after the divorce.

Does this suggest that divorce is only a short-term crisis and that kids are better off if you leave your marriage? Not entirely.

Yongmin Sun and Yuanzhang Li found that academic test scores continued to decline. One reason for this is that once kids get behind in class it can be difficult to catch up.

This, in turn, could lead to low motivation and lack of confidence.

After tracking 1,400 divorced families, including 2,500 children, for up to 30 years, Mavis Hetherington and her team found that a small minority of kids of divorced parents suffered permanently from the experience. They did have around twice as many emotional, social, behavioural and educational problems as youngsters whose parents stay together, but she, too, suggests that many of the problems may have been present before the divorce.

She also notes that after getting over the initial disruption, most youngsters adjusted to their new circumstances and developed into reasonably well-adjusted individuals.

When Diana, Princess of Wales, was asked in a BBC TV interview, 'What were the expectations that you had for married life?' she responded, 'I think like any marriage, specially when you've had divorced parents like myself, you'd want to try even harder to make it work and you don't want to fall back into a pattern that you've seen happen in your own family.'

This is a common view among children of divorced parents. Most say they will delay having children until they're sure their own marriages are rock solid. They don't want to put their own kids through the painful experiences they had.

While many children of divorced couples do have successful marriages, the census data from a number of western countries suggests they do indeed have a higher risk of marriage failure. Perhaps this is because they didn't learn good relationship skills from their parents. Sadly, Diana, Princess of Wales, was one of these statistics.

As well as the impact on the children, you'll need to consider the intense emotions separated parents have over their offspring.

One vivid memory I have is of a man in his late thirties handing his two youngsters a bag of presents and then kissing them goodbye at a bus stop. 'Thanks, Daddy. Wish you could be with us too', said the older one. He watched as they climbed aboard and waved to him from the bus window until it turned a corner. He then burst into tears. It was Christmas Eve and it was obvious the children were going to spend Christmas with their mother. Silently, I said a short prayer asking God to be with this man and his family during this painful time in their lives. I little knew that on Christmas Eve 20 years later, I would be in a similar position to that man.

Fathers sometimes pay for their children without getting the same opportunity to be parents. These dads say this is to the detriment of their kids, who need an adult male role model. Children can also feel increasingly estranged from their fathers. Over time, fathers may feel superfluous and visits drop off dramatically. Contact with their kids can virtually cease when the children reach late teens or if the father relocates to a different town.

For whatever reason, many fathers give reduced financial contributions or avoid paying child support. This can result in the mother needing to take on extra employment or getting by on government and charitable handouts. Most find this demeaning. It may also leave the children feeling abandoned.

It can be hard enough bringing up children in a two-parent family; could you cope as a solo parent? Will it affect your ability to take paid employment? Do you want your kids in childcare? Is childcare available and can you afford it? What if you can't afford babysitters and must therefore forgo the chance to have a social life, including dating? What happens if you're sick? If you have teenagers, what kind of controls can you place on their behaviour when you're not at home? What happens if one of your kids wants to switch custody arrangements in a few years' time? And how will your children fit into any future relationships that you or your spouse may have – especially if your new partners have families of their own?

Looking at the situation objectively, you might decide that you'd be happier leaving the relationship, but the children would be adversely affected for some time. So, where to now?

Legal firms and agencies specializing in family and marriage law provide advice on legal questions. Counsellors, mediators, and other agencies specializing in the family will also help you to examine in detail your particular issues.

The Future happiness and unhappiness tables (Tables 9.1 and 9.2) in the next chapter are designed to help you weigh up the benefits and risks that go with making your decision.

9

Deciding your future

————◆·◆·◆————

Assessing your future

The following process is designed to help you become aware of your chances for happiness.

Set up two tables: one for future happiness and the other for future unhappiness, as shown in the example of Jenny's answers.

Ask God to help you answer honestly and gain insight through your answers.

Jot down a few key words and phrases that sum up the answer to the questions. Write what first comes to mind, as that is more likely to be what matters to you. Concentrate on specific answers relating to what will bring long-term contentment or long-term discontent rather than temporary feelings of euphoria or sadness. If you're stuck or uncertain about how to respond, think of what has happened in the past as this will be a good guide to what may happen in the future.

Limit yourself to three key answers for each question. This helps to focus on what you think is important. If you change your mind and think of a different answer later, decide which is the least important of your answers, and if necessary replace a previous answer with the new one.

In the last two columns, circle or highlight the answer you think is most correct.

Try to resist answers you think others will find acceptable or that you're embarrassed to expose – like a desire to spend more time away from the children or have casual relationships.

Guide to filling in the Future happiness table
(Table 9.1)

Needs

Your needs can be spiritual, physical, emotional, intellectual, social or economic. Be specific, like a need to spend more time with friends or a partner who will be more compatible with your personality and interests.

How would you meet the needs you've identified?

Jot down what you plan to do. If you want to spend more time with your children, you might note that you need to reschedule your work time or plan to look for a job which is more family-friendly, maybe something part-time or closer to the children's school.

What risks do you face?

Note what can stand in the way of meeting your needs. It could be fears for your safety, lack of training, lack of funds, your age, few potential partners, no local job openings and so on.

How would you reduce the risk?

Reflect on practical ways you could reduce the risk so that you increase your chances of success. If you've remarked that there are likely to be no jobs that are family-friendly, maybe you could make a note to research the possibility of working from home or trying another career.

What are your chances of success?

The score ranges from 0, where the chances of success are low or very unlikely, to 5, where the chances of success are very high. If you need to leave your partner for safety and there's the opportunity to set up a new home in another town, then rate the chances of success as 5. If you fear your partner will track you down, or escape is difficult, you might rate your chances as 0.

Are your chances better if you stay or go?

This might be difficult to answer. If you want more intimacy and communication from a partner, you may want to leave your spouse and look for someone more suitable. But if you rate your chances of success of finding a Mr or Ms Right as low, then you may be an 'Unsure'. Choose what, on balance, seems the best answer.

How important to you?

Rank what you think is the key to your happiness over both tables. Score what matters most with 1 and what matters least with 18. You can rate two or more answers at the same level.

Guide to filling in the Future unhappiness table (Table 9.2)

Fill in the Future unhappiness table in much the same way as the Future happiness table. The only difference is that the scenarios are situations or circumstances that will cause you unhappiness. Score your chances of success by how you rate your chances of avoiding these scenarios. If you fear your partner will win custody of your children and turn them against you, and you've suggested discussing this with him or her and hiring a lawyer to reduce the risk, you might rate your chances of avoiding your fear as reasonable and give it a score of 3 or 4.

Reviewing your answers

When you've filled out the two tables put them aside. This gives you a chance to think about how you've answered the questions. About once a week over the next two months review what you've written, offer it to God in prayer and spend time in silence listening to what God might be saying to you, then make any changes that better reflect what you think God wants.

Note the date you change an answer and try to explain the reason briefly. This could reveal a pattern emerging, and give insight into your motives and feelings about the future. Whatever changes you make, ask yourself: 'What has happened since I last reviewed my answers to make me want to make this change?'

The sample answers below are from Jenny, the wife from the Relationship assessment in Chapter 6, pp. 76–89. Again, they are hypothetical and used as a guide to how to set up and fill out your own tables. You'll have different experiences from those in the sample, so your answers will be different.

Scoring

Your chances of success?

Add and combine the score in the 'Your chances of success?' column in both tables. If you rated all 18 answers with 5 then your score would be the maximum of 90. And if you scored all your chances at 3 then the score would be 54.

Are your chances better if you stay or go?

Add the total number of answers in both tables in the 'Are your chances better if you stay or go?' column that you've circled with Stay, Go and Unsure. For example, you might have rated 10 of your answers as Stay, 4 as Go and 4 as Unsure.

How important to you?

You've already rated your answers by how important they are to you from 1 to 18.

How sound are your results?

How reliable?

One important check on your reliability is how often you changed your mind when you reviewed your answers over the two-month period. The results are more reliable if changes are minor rather than major rethinks.

If you made major changes and the points you raised were what you were thinking at the time you wrote them but you're still unsure, it's worth going back to your tables and continuing to record your

Table 9.1 Future happiness table

Question	Needs	How would you meet these needs?	What risks do you face?	How will you reduce the risk?	Your chances of success? 0 = low 5 = high	Are your chances better if you stay or go?	How important to you? Rank from 1 to 18 (both tables)
1 What do you need to make you happy for the next 5+ years?	Financial certainty.	Find full-time work.	Lack of qualifications. Age discrimination.	Get a CV together. Choose and contact potential referees.	0 1 2 3 **4** 5	Stay **Go** Unsure	5
	Physical safety.	Leave my husband.	He'll injure me.	Get a secure home with a garage.	0 1 2 3 **4** 5	Stay **Go** Unsure	1
	Friends.	Cultivate new friendships.	Old friends will fall away or be hard to keep.	This will be hard to go through. Just be myself.	0 **1** 2 3 4 5	Stay **Go** Unsure	13

Table 9.1 (continued)

Question	Needs	How would you meet these needs?	What risks do you face?	How will you reduce the risk?	Your chances of success? 0 = low 5 = high	Are your chances better if you stay or go?	How important to you? Rank from 1 to 18 (both tables)
2 What do your children (or others you have a close relationship with) need for their happiness for the next 5+ years?	Emotional stability.	Keep everyday life as normal as possible.	Blame. Burnout. Blowing the budget.	It will be tempting to compete with their father.	0 1 2 ③ 4 5	Stay **Go** Unsure	3
	A place to call home.	Find a home.	Legal hurdles releasing money.	Get a good lawyer and estate agent.	0 1 2 3 ④ 5	Stay **Go** Unsure	14
	Personal achievement.	Identify what they're good at, enrol them, take them.	Stretching the budget. Burnout.	Make it a priority for them. It will also take me out of myself.	0 1 2 3 4 ⑤	Stay **Go** Unsure	10

3 What does your spouse need for his or her happiness for the next 5 years?						
Get a life.	I've tried. It's now up to him.	Shame. Blame.	Remember he may not want to be happy.	(0) 1 2 3 4 5	Stay Go Unsure	17
Being able to control others.	Others doesn't mean me.	He may still want to control me by at least holding out financially, at most harming me.	Pray he'll find someone else soon – but not to abuse.	(0) 1 2 3 4 5	Stay Go Unsure	18
Money.	Can't.	He'll try to get my share, as he has tried to already.	Cut minor losses. More important to get free.	(0) 1 2 3 4 5	Stay Go Unsure	7

Table 9.2 Future unhappiness table

Question	Scenarios	How would you avoid these scenarios happening?	What risks do you face?	How will you reduce the risk?	Your chances of success? 0 = low 5 = high	Are your chances better if you stay or go?	How important to you? Rank from 1 to 18 (both tables)
1 What would make you unhappy for the next 5+ years?	Ill health.	Get out of the marriage now before health problems become chronic.	Injury at his hand instead.	Have faith and keep positive. Keep motivated. Don't waver from what I've decided to do.	0 1 2 3 (4) 5	Stay (Go) Unsure	12
	Not being able to see my children every day.	Get a job where I can have more contact with them.	Meeting with my husband all the time.	Ask around. Have faith and keep positive.	0 1 2 (3) 4 5	Stay (Go) Unsure	8

				0 1 2 ③ 4 5	Stay ⟨Go⟩ Unsure	6
Losing financially in the marriage settlement.	Get a good lawyer.	Confronting his family and their lawyers.	I may have to share a flat rather than buy a house – try to minimize the effect on the kids.			
2 What would make your children (or others you have a close relationship with) unhappy for the next 5+ years? The marriage split itself.	Make sure they know they're loved and it's not their fault.	They'll believe their father.	I have to live with this. One day they'll learn the truth.	0 ① 2 3 4 5	Stay ⟨Go⟩ Unsure	2
Leaving the house they grew up in.	Bring lots of familiar things, especially toys, to make the new place home.	It will be a drop in lifestyle and a contrast to their father's place.	Remember having a loving home is all that counts.	0 1 2 3 4 ⑤	Stay ⟨Go⟩ Unsure	11
Dealing with my and their father's issues.	Try not to criticize the other party in front of them.	Pouring it all out to a friend in the children's presence.	It's hard as I'm human!	0 1 2 ③ 4 5	Stay ⟨Go⟩ Unsure	15

Table 9.2 (continued)

Question	Scenarios	How would you avoid these scenarios happening?	What risks do you face?	How will you reduce the risk?	Your chances of success? 0 = low 5 = high	Are your chances better if you stay or go?	How important to you? Rank from 1 to 18 (both tables)
3 What would make your spouse unhappy for the next 5 years?	Something happening to the children.	Be careful.	Maybe blame but he accepts I'm a good mother.	Try to keep our mutual love of the kids as a bridge to communication.	0 1 2 3 4 (5)	Stay (Go) Unsure	4
	His mother's death.	I'm too far removed to have any influence.	Maybe abuse for not liking her enough.	Rather not.	0 1 2 3 4 (5)	Stay (Go) Unsure	9
	Successful business competitor, tax audit.	Keep my mouth shut.	Anything I say will be construed as worse disloyalty than leaving him!	It's behind me already, including the ethical issues that bugged me.	0 1 2 3 4 (5)	Stay (Go) Unsure.	16
Score (Both tables combined)					55 (Max = 90)	Stay = 0 Go = 17 Unsure = 1	

points honestly over the next few months until there's a relatively consistent pattern from weekly entries over a whole month.

How valid?

Check the credibility of what you've written with someone whose judgement you can trust, but not your spouse at this stage. If you know you're going to show your assessment to your partner that could influence your answers.

A wise friend might confirm what you've written, suggest other points you've missed or challenge your assessments. He or she might also ask probing questions to help you understand some of your underlying motives and biases.

As a result of your discussions, ask again for God's guidance and make any changes to your tables that you consider valid. But don't treat the tables as the definitive word or use them or the methods you've applied as a weapon against your partner. God might have other plans for you.

What do your results mean?

Your chances of success

Although this is not a scientific test, the way you've rated your chances of success gives an insight into how optimistic you are about your future happiness.

Table 9.3 Future happiness and unhappiness scores

Score	Comments
70–90	You're generally optimistic but it's worth noting any low scores. For instance, you might rate your chances of attaining happiness high for yourself and your children, but low for your partner.
50–69	You're hovering between optimism and pessimism. Take special note of any high or low scores. Maybe you're optimistic about some of your goals and pessimistic about others.
0–49	This suggests pessimism over your future happiness. You could also be feeling depressed and overwhelmed by feelings of despair. Nevertheless, take special note of any answer that you've rated as having a high chance of success.

Are your chances better if you stay or go?

Add up how many times you've circled Stay compared with Go or Unsure. You'll probably find that there's a clear pattern in favour of either staying or going, with some Unsures. For example, if you had a score of 13 Stays, 3 Unsures and 2 Gos, then it would indicate that, on balance, you believe that you'd be happier staying.

How important to you?

Not all answers are of equal importance. Look especially at the first four or five most highly ranked responses. These indicate what's uppermost on your mind. If you think your partner is dependent on you, or you're concerned for his or her future, you might well rate your partner's needs as very important.

Like many questionnaires, especially a subjective one like this, the greatest benefit comes from filling out the answers. It brings to the surface what you deem important to your future and helps clarify how you might achieve it.

Jenny's answers

Jenny's answers indicate she has virtually made up her mind to leave her partner. She has chosen Go in answer to 17 of the 18 questions. Her only hesitation is about whether the children will still feel loved and convinced it's not their fault.

Jenny is less sure about her chances of success. Her total score is a mid-range 55 out of a maximum of 90. She is most pessimistic about her spouse. She rates her ability to help him meet his needs as zero, yet rates her chances of reducing his future unhappiness as high. Otherwise she is generally optimistic. Her main concerns are about making friends and how the children will react.

The order in which she ranks her responses is revealing, especially the first five.

These are about her own and the children's safety, along with her need for emotional and financial stability. Many of her lower-ranked answers echo these themes.

Decision time

Do you meet the three principle criteria for leaving your marriage?

1 The marriage has broken down.
2 The marriage can't be salvaged.
3 A split would provide greater prospects for long-term happiness.

Your assessments help you make up your mind. If they show your marriage has broken down for valid reasons (see Chapter 5, p. 55, and Chapter 6, p. 75), that the marriage can't be salvaged (see Chapter 7, p. 90) and that you'd be happier leaving (Chapter 8, p. 104, and pp. 117–28 above), then this would suggest leaving your partner. Likewise, if your assessments show that there's hope for your marriage and that you'd be happier staying, then this points to your staying.

But before you come to a definite decision, pray again for God's guidance. Jesus and St Paul urge us to have faith and be persistent in prayer. We need to persevere, but not because God is forgetful and needs a constant reminder or because our prayers have a short use-by date. Nor is it a question of continuing to pester God until our prayers rise to the top of the pile of his 'to-do list'. It's so we can remain continually open to his direction.

Decisions are not always straightforward. What happens if only one or two of the three principles apply to your situation? Maybe your marriage is beyond repair, yet you'll be unhappy if you leave. For instance, you might be in a loveless marriage, but if you leave, it's almost certain you'll be lonely, live at subsistence level, the children will suffer and you'll see less of them.

Similarly, while your marriage may be bearable, you consider you and your partner stand a better chance of happiness if you go your separate ways. For example, you might find a partner who's keen on having the children you desperately desire or already has kids from a previous relationship.

If there's no clear pointer to whether you should stay or quit your relationship, then consider staying until you have a clearer idea of your future relationship and happiness. Be aware, though, that your indecisiveness may affect adversely the way you treat your partner and children. Be open to the Holy Spirit's guidance.

Shall I go?

Even when the decision is clear cut, as it is in the example of Jenny above, you may still have reservations. It's normal to feel anxious about thinking of leaving a spouse. In a way, you're admitting defeat. While this may be the best course of action, it's not what most of us want or what we expect to do.

These honourable feelings of resistance need to be weighed against what your marriage has become. Captains who abandon their sinking ships can also feel bad about deserting their posts – even though they have done the right thing. It's unlikely God would want us to stay in a very unhappy marriage out of a stubborn sense of duty or out of pride when all that can reasonably be done to repair the relationship has been done and there's no good reason to stay. Christianity is about putting the past behind us and moving on reborn to a new abundant life in God.

If you've placed the decision on hold because you fear loneliness or nasty unforeseen happenings, you will need to face this honestly and pray for guidance. Take your time to be certain: your gut instincts might be the Holy Spirit's way of telling you to think it through again.

Shall I stay?

You may just as easily feel qualms about staying – even though it's the best solution. Your assessments might indicate your marriage is salvageable and that you and your family would be happier staying together. Yet, you still have a hankering to go.

Despite the odds being stacked against your leaving, you feel like leaving your mundane marriage for an adventure. Possibly, you're one of those contrary people who feel uncomfortable when they're happy. These feelings, too, can be irrational.

You may need time to bring these issues into the open and work through them so you can let your heart and emotions catch up with your reasoning. Again, a wise friend, counsellor or Christian advisor may be able to help by acting as a sounding board to let you reflect on what's bothering you. It's also worth remembering that there are nearly always losses and gains no matter what decision you make and the answer lies in working out what's best on balance.

Maybe you need to make a decision and move ahead in faith.

10

Leaving

Minimum distress

If you've decided to leave your spouse, then the fourth principle (see p. 54) applies: The separation needs to be just, fair and cause the minimum of distress. For Christians this means the separation needs to be a witness to God's healing love for all.

You might feel you don't care what happens to your partner. But ignoring this fourth principle is a sure recipe for creating ongoing problems and distress. It's also a poor witness to your Christian faith.

'I'm leaving you'

There's no easy way to tell your spouse you want to leave your marriage, especially if he or she still loves you. Ambushing your partner with a pre-emptive 'I'm leaving you' as you're about to walk out the door will avoid protracted exits, but even if your spouse knows you're unhappy and might possibly welcome your decision, it will still come as a shock.

> It happened 11 years ago. I arrived home from work to find my wife, April, had packed my bags and they were down in the entrance hall. She announced, 'I'm through with you and our marriage. The taxi is coming to take you to the Camelot Hotel. I've reserved a room for you. My lawyer will be in touch tomorrow.' I felt sick. When the taxi arrived, a man got out with a couple of suitcases. April made certain I knew what he meant to her. 'That's Joe, my lover, he's living here now.' We passed each other on the driveway. It was a terrible, humiliating experience and I'm still suffering.

Liam was so shocked, he did what April wanted. Although he dated several women after that, he said he felt so angry and depressed by what April had done to him that he couldn't trust them enough to have a close relationship. He died a year after he told me his story, leaving much of his wealth to his former wife who, after living with several men, was now on her own. At his graveside, she shed tears of remorse and asked for forgiveness.

How you communicate your decision is an important witness to your faith. It can affect the way your partner, your children and others view you. It can also set the tone for the relationship you have with them after you leave. Here are some guidelines:

- Plan when and how to end the relationship so it causes minimum distress and problems.
- Make it clear that the relationship has broken down, not the individuals involved. Avoid blaming yourself or your partner, even if you believe there is fault.
- State clearly what you've decided so there are no misunderstandings.
- Point out to your partner how you're seeking to negotiate a just-and-fair settlement. This may include a suggested timeline and agenda for negotiations, such as the date when you part, sale of assets, division of joint wealth, child custody arrangements and so on.
- Try to understand your partner's reactions, including disbelief and grief over the ending of the relationship. Respect his or her views, even if you strongly disagree.
- State what you want to do next and ask your partner if that is acceptable or whether he or she wants to make an alternative suggestion. You might also suggest both of you undertaking counselling to exit the relationship. This could include discussing the issues that came between you in order to help you both in any future relationships.

Your children

- Assure them that you both still love them and will continue to care and look after them.

- Explain that the relationship between you has broken down because of your incompatibly, not because of them. Don't describe the details or involve them in your disputes.
- Consult with them if this is appropriate, but don't expect them to make decisions about your lives or custody and visiting arrangements.
- To help reduce their anxiety, tell them what's going to happen and how you plan to look after their interests.
- As far as possible, maintain familiar rules and routines in their lives.
- It may be worth suggesting they talk to an independent person, such as a grandparent, who can listen and help them cope.
- Don't overcompensate out of guilt or allow them to use the situation to manipulate you to get their own way.

A just-and-fair separation

No matter how considerate you are in letting your partner know you're leaving, a break-up is fraught with emotion and feelings of unfairness. In one study, only about a fifth of former husbands and a third of ex-wives said the outcome was fair. Most thought it fair in some ways and not in others.

A just-and-fair division of assets may mean dividing and sharing things evenly or according to some other formula; or each of you taking what belongs to you, such as personal items and your share of what you jointly own; or getting what you deserve, so that, if you gave up your career to look after the children, you deserve recognition for this in the separation agreement.

Perhaps you believe you deserve more because you're the injured party who has had to put up with a lot of bad behaviour. Your spouse, in contrast, may think you're unreasonable for not wanting to divide everything down the middle.

It's easy to see how the separation process could become a battleground, with claims, counterclaims and legal threats. There might be attempts to conceal information and wealth. Recriminations, character assassination and trying to turn the children against the other parent are common tactics.

In contrast, some partners don't bother about their own interests. In their grief, they may no longer care what happens and back off from anything that reminds them of the marriage. They may insist on immediately selling the jointly owned home and taking a loss instead of waiting until it's a seller's market. They may feel guilty for causing the split, want to be generous because they still love their partner, or they may simply give in to pressure.

If you do this, you may come to regret it later, especially if you're disadvantaged as a result.

> I felt she deserved the home for the sake of the kids as she had prime custody. Six months after we divorced, she met this rich guy, sold our house and lived in his mansion. Now they're talking of marriage. I'm not bitter, but if I'd known my ex would do that, I wouldn't have been so charitable.

This was how one man described to me how he felt a year after their divorce.

Aim for an agreement that will avoid disadvantaging yourself to such a degree, while still taking into consideration the special circumstances of your spouse and children. Perhaps this couple could have come to an arrangement where she got the use of the home, rather than outright ownership, until the kids left home or her situation changed.

We sometimes think of a just agreement as one that meets legal requirements. But this doesn't always mean it's going to be fair to you, your partner or your children. Fairness implies natural justice rather than legal justice. For example, many years ago you may have set up a private trust to invest some of your income and avoid its being legally included in any separation settlement. The money is yours (and whoever else benefits from your trust funds) and you might legally be entitled to this money, but is this fair to your spouse?

Guidelines for how to separate

In the same way that you both agreed to marry, it's worth trying to agree together on how you'll separate. Otherwise, your partner might accuse you of setting the agenda to your own advantage.

If you're to do this face to face with your partner, try to communicate with each other in a mature, rational way. Offer a point of view, listen to your spouse and respond clearly and, if necessary, make an effort to reach a compromise.

You and your partner may each want your own support person present when you discuss your separation. A support person acts as an observer, helps you to understand what is happening and reminds you to keep calm and stay focused.

If there are legal issues to sort out, you may need to hire a lawyer. Your spouse should have a different legal advisor to avoid conflict of interest. Your lawyer will aim to look after your best interests. He or she will explain your legal rights and duties and arrange for family assets you have a claim on to be audited and valued, help you meet legal requirements and put forward your case in disputes. This may include filing divorce papers or preparing a separation agreement. If necessary, your lawyer will represent you in court. The court may also appoint a lawyer or other official experienced in family disputes to act for the interests of your children, especially if there is a custody dispute.

There are disadvantages. Working through lawyers can make the process adversarial and remote. Many view divorce lawyers as having self-interest in prolonging cases by raising technicalities and dwelling on moot points of detail. Jesus warns of the importance of settling matters with an adversary because of the cost involved in going to court (Matt. 5.25).

Many couples complain that legal processes are inflexible and intimidating. Their feelings and views seem to be of secondary importance. Court decisions are sometimes criticized for reflecting middle-class conservative values, especially over childcare. You may also find yourself tied down to a contract that will require your returning to the legal process if you wish to make changes.

If you plan to use legal advisors, check first on their reputation and style of practice. Will they listen and take your advice? Is their style confrontational or conciliatory, and so on? This will help you to choose professionals who are compatible with your method of separating. Make certain you're aware beforehand of likely costs and what each fee covers, or put a cap on the amount you're willing to pay. Otherwise, you could get a big shock when you receive the bill – at a time when you'll most likely be taking a drop in your standard of living.

An alternative process for deciding separation disputes is to use a mediator who specializes in families. Check the Yellow Pages, law firms, the internet and organizations that offer interpersonal services to couples, such as Relate. A mediator doesn't usually act as a judge who will decide the issues that come between you: he or she guides you to make a suitable decision yourselves.

Many couples begin by sorting out what they want to do as individuals, alone or with the help of a mediator. They then get their respective solicitors to check and advise on the solutions they have reached together, to draw up a final agreement and handle the legal side of the divorce. The advantage is that you're keeping your legal costs down by using only the professional services you really need.

If you and your partner can face each other amicably, there may be little reason to involve others. Most couples are capable of agreeing on a just-and-fair solution, including care of children. If you're certain you want a divorce, check with your local family court to find out what's involved and consider doing it yourselves. There are other organizations and many websites that offer advice for couples who want to make their own legal agreement. Check them out under 'Divorce' in the Yellow Pages or through an internet search. Pray for God's guidance.

If you and your spouse are willing to discuss face to face how you'll separate, then establish some ground rules, such as:

- agreeing to the scope and agenda for each meeting and sticking to this;
- total honesty and transparency;
- equal opportunity to present each other's views;
- listening to and respecting each other's point of view, including those of your children if that is applicable;
- avoiding blame or comments about the reasons for the break-up;

- establishing methods for handling disputes and when to use a support person, mediator, lawyers or the courts;
- establishing what happens if one of you doesn't stick to the separation agreement;
- checking that all relevant issues are adequately discussed;
- agreeing in writing to accept decisions and not to renegotiate them unless there's a change in circumstances or an obvious mistake.

Separation tables

After you've agreed to ground rules, consider using tables like the sample ones below to help you come to important decisions. They provide a record of what you've decided, how you'll put these decisions into practice and any other relevant comments. Don't forget to pray for guidance to know what God wants for you both, rather than what you want.

List money, assets and other things you have in common or have as a claim on one another. Include the care and upbringing of any children (see also section below, 'What about the kids?', p. 139). Consider pets.

Next, list the key issues that need to be decided. This may include both long- and short-term needs, such as financial support while one of you retrains for the workforce or provision for your children's welfare at different stages of their growth.

Group these issues in three tables headed 'Easy', 'Possible' and 'Challenging'. You'll probably find it easy to decide to keep the clothes you wear, so clothes will go in the 'Easy' table. It's likely that you'll come to a compromise over your CD and DVD collections. Maybe you'll divide the collections by drawing lots and therefore add this decision to the 'Compromise' table. It could be very challenging to decide who has prime custodial care of a family pet. As you could both be determined to claim the pet, this issue would belong in the 'Challenging' table.

Try to avoid nitpicking over the cost of possessions. Your spouse might have a more extensive and therefore expensive wardrobe but, unless it's excessive, does that really matter?

Then record your solution, how the solution is going to be implemented, whom it applies to and when it will apply. Under 'Comments', note any issues, conditions, or other comments that are pertinent. For subjects that are difficult and challenging to settle between you, it's worth recording each of your views.

The three sample tables, 10.1a, 10.1b and 10.1c, present three issues, their solutions and implementation. Jim and Mary, our hypothetical couple from Chapter 7, pp. 98–100, have decided to part. This is how they filled in the tables.

If you can't decide on something, ask yourself: why is this issue so important to my future happiness? Look for innovative solutions. If you've already agreed to have equal custody of the children but can't agree on who gets them over weekends, then suggest alternating every month. Or the one who has them during the week could have them for the longer summer break.

Once you've finished the tables, put them aside, pray about them and recheck them together several days later. Sign and date them when you finally agree, thereby putting the process into effect.

What about your kids?

Who'll take care of your kids and how? Even though you and your spouse are breaking up, you're still their parents. You'll probably both agree that your children are the best legacy of your marriage. Neither of you will want them to suffer because of your split.

Chapter 8 outlines the effects of divorce on children. In general, kids suffer from the worsening relationship between their parents before, as well as after, the split. They have a higher chance of emotional and behavioural problems and poorer school grades than children whose parents stay together. Nevertheless, most children learn to cope with the experience and adjust reasonably well.

We are aware of the worse-case scenarios that create the maximum distress: creating obstacles for the other parent, legal battles over custody and poisoning children against the other parent – even abducting them.

Table 10.1 Separation tables

a Easy

Issue	Solution	How	Who	When	Comments
Clothes and personal items.	Keep own clothes and take responsibility for them. Not valued for separation.	Each partner to sort and pack own clothes. Both to do children's clothes.	Jim and Mary.	When each leaves for new accommodation.	Children need separate clothes for temporary stay with grandparents.
Computer equipment.	To go to Jim.	Jim to take possession after Mary makes copies of her files.	Jim.	As soon as possible.	It's a near-new computer of similar value to old car.
Car.	To go to Mary.	Jim to sign over joint ownership to Mary. Mary to get documentation.	Mary.	Before Jim leaves for new accommodation.	Old car of similar value to near-new computer.

b Compromise

Issue	Solution	How	Who	When	Comments
Commercial CDs, DVDs and videos.	Evenly divided.	Every second one in the stack, flipping a coin to see who starts.	Jim and Mary.	Leaving for new accommodation.	Can agree to swap if either gets something they don't like which the other wants.
Family photos and family videos.	Agree to select what each wants or make copies for the other.	Joint funds to pay for copies.	Jim to arrange copies of photos, Mary to copy videos.	As soon as possible.	Family history important for children.
Who will organize selling family home?	Both equally.	Four estate agents to provide estimate and marketing plans.	Both to contact two estate agents.	Early spring to maximize price.	If can't agree on which agency, go with more than one.

Table 10.1 (continued)

c Challenging

Issue	Jim's view	Mary's view	Solution	How	Who	When	Comments
Custody of the dog.	One who usually feeds it and plays with it. Great companion.	One who usually takes it for walks and to vet. Will be a guard dog when I go solo.	Both want dog so need to work on sharing arrangement. Electronic security for Jenny so guard dog not crucial.	Month in each home with 'walking the dog' privileges for the other on prior request.	Both.	After the last person is relocated.	New accommodation for one partner may not allow pets. May need to renegotiate visiting/ walking rights.
Valuable art work.	Saw its value and bought it. Would fetch good price to help us both.	Emotionally attached. Rather starve then sell.	To be valued and half value to be paid by Mary, who will then own it on final separation.	The mean between two independent valuations.	Each to organize their art valuation.	As socn as possible.	That the cost will be too high for Mary. May need to concede ownership of other items to help pay.

Whether Mary can still use married surname.	As she's leaving me, it's hypocritical to keep using my family name.	Name by which I'm known at work and for official purposes. A huge job to change. Also good to have the same name as the children.	Jim can only view it as a request as Mary doesn't have to change her name and doesn't want to.	Request noted and will be reviewed if Mary remarries.	Mary.	Can review at any time and especially if Mary remarries.	May want to see what the children think.

I received a call from a distraught father I used to work with in the USA. He remembered his former wife once saying she would like to emigrate to New Zealand, where I was born and now live. He was trying desperately to locate her and their daughter who had disappeared several years before. I put him in contact with the authorities who specialize in international family abductions, but there was no evidence they had come to New Zealand. In such sad cases, the motive is often revenge or a belief that the other parent has nothing good to offer the kids. Parents can transfer their bitterness towards their ex to the children, making any future relationship, let alone reconciliation, with the abandoned parent nigh on impossible.

The belief that break-ups are adult matters from which children need shielding is at the other extreme. No matter how old we are, life can throw up disappointments and events beyond our control. People fall out with one another and children need to come to understand this in a way that is suitable for them. They can learn that, even in the midst of pain and broken dreams, you both continue to love them.

The way you relate to each other and care for your children is a model for them. If you fight with your partner and are inconsistent with the kids, then that's how they'll handle their own relationships, thus perpetuating a cycle of unhappiness. It's also a poor witness to God's reconciling love.

How do you decide which of you should look after the kids? For most, the answer seems obvious. Children, especially very young ones, need their mother. Although – with the exception of breastfeeding – men are indeed capable of nurturing their young, society mostly expects a dad to be the breadwinner and a mum to be the caregiver. This can be unfair to dads.

Not all parents want to be involved in the everyday care of their kids after a break-up and may prefer joint custody or a visitation arrangement. Sometimes children are split between parents, such as the older ones going with their dad and the younger ones with their mum. You may want to care for them now and then hand them over to your ex later, or vice versa. And what your kids want may be different from what you or your ex wants. There are many possibilities.

Before going into battle for custody, think carefully about how you, and your ex, would meet your children's needs. This includes love and affection; education; living and financial arrangements; visiting and access rights; the demands of your work, your recreational and social life; providing care when the children are sick or on holiday and how you'd handle any future disputes about their upbringing.

While telling me how concerned he was by his daughter's behaviour, a Christian father confessed that he and his ex hadn't established ways of resolving such problems.

> Her mother has put our 16-year-old Julie on the pill and lets her boyfriend sleep over because she thinks it's better they do it at home than in the backseat of a car. I don't agree with that and won't allow it to happen when Julie comes to my place. Julie's told me to go to hell and she'll stay with her mum instead.

Julie did decide to stay with her mother – until her boyfriend left her for someone else. She then spent time with her father until she got another boyfriend. She was playing each parent to suit herself, which only heightened the conflict between them.

To avoid, or at least reduce, disputes like this, it may help if you and your ex set up a table like tables 10.2a and 10.2b (Meeting your children's needs), which is what Julie's parents eventually did. Begin by asking God to help you do what is best for your family and then list each child's main needs, how best to meet them, the issues that may arise and how you'll resolve them. You may need to do this separately and then look to how you can reach a compromise. If your kids are old enough, you may want their input. But they need to realize it's not the same as filling out a birthday present wish list. You may also seek the help of a support person, a family counsellor or mediator. Some parents place more emphasis on their kids' education than other needs. Don't forget to include emotional, social, spiritual, moral and recreational needs. Allow for renegotiation if there's a change of circumstances, such as one of you relocating to another town or marrying again.

Add as many rows as you need and use a separate table for each child. Here's a sample of how our hypothetical couple Mary and Jim

Table 10.2 Meeting your children's needs

a Donna

Donna's needs	How best met	Resources required	Who	When	Issues	How they'll be resolved
To pass her exams.	Privacy.	Her own room, desk and study area.	Both households ensure this.	As soon as possible.	Hero-worshipping Mary's new boyfriend's daughter, who wants to share a room and watch TV together.	New 'step-sister' gets to keep Donna's TV in her room till the exams are over.
To spend time with her grandparents (mother's parents).	Spend a night a week at their place.	Transport.	The parent she's with drops her off. Grandfather takes her to school the next day.	Tuesdays – unless other activities intervene. Then arrange another day.	Father's parents, whom Donna finds boring, wanting equal time.	Arrange family outing with father's parents so everyone helps out.

A place for the pet pony.	Hiring a stall at a stable.	Good care/access/a big paddock to run in. (No room at either house – both parents have to downgrade residences.)	Urgent.	Donna to investigate and decide herself.	Who pays? How to break it to Donna if no one can afford this.	May need to call a meeting with the wider family to share cost. May need to consider selling the pony.
Counselling.	Get referrals from school and youth agencies.	Information.	When she's ready.	Donna has to decide.	At this point, she doesn't want counselling but is showing signs of anxiety.	In the first instance, talk to her teachers to see what the school can do.

Table 10.2 (continued)

b Sam

Sam's needs	How best met	Resources required	Who	When	Issues	How they'll be resolved
Role models.	Meeting new people through clubs, sport, kids group at church.	Transport.	Both parents/ school.	Soon.	He's shy. Lacks direction. Low self-esteem. Finds his father difficult.	More through maturity and the passage of time than from forcing it. Father needs to step back from the situation for now.
Motivation to be interested in school.	Minimizing peer pressure to opt out and underachieve.	Supervision.	School. Parents – for homework.	Immediate.	Parents are both busy and it's hard to monitor Sam as he goes from household to household.	More communication between parents and with the school. Sam must report in about his schoolwork.

| Counselling. | Get referrals from school and youth agencies. | Information. | Sam says he's depressed and wants to have counselling. Both parents to set up. | Soon. | May not want to face the problems with his father if they come up in counselling. | Ultimately, it's up to him. |
| A pet (something to love)? | Kittens readily available. | Minimal. | Sam to choose. | Fairly soon. | Donna may be upset because of issues over pony. | Talk to the children – then just do it! |

filled out the tables for their two children, 11-year-old Donna and 8-year-old Sam, to accommodate new circumstances and avoid unpleasant surprises.

Mary and Jim are aware that some of Donna's and Sam's behaviour is normal. It's part of growing up and not related to the split. But even 8-year-old Sam recognizes he's depressed, displaying low motivation and difficulty relating to his father. They agree that Jim may need to step back for a while and that Mary and Jim both need to keep in close touch with the school, maybe seek counselling and give Sam the opportunity to relate to other role models. The possibility of losing her pony is causing Donna's anxiety, not the break-up at this stage, but she will blame the break-up, and resent her parents, if the pony is sold because of financial hardship.

Most kids criticize their parents for not giving in to their demands in ordinary circumstances, let alone the extraordinary. Help your children make adjustments. Though hard at the time, it can be part of their learning experience.

Agree that neither of you will try to do anything that will hurt the kids or alienate them from either of you, such as:

- blaming your children for the break-up or using them as scapegoats;
- withholding visiting rights or a child's reasonable desire to telephone, text, email or write to their other parent;
- undermining any of the children or their other parent, even if the kids take sides with your ex;
- allowing the children to undermine each other or a parent, or allowing them to refuse to visit their other parent when it's that parent's turn, without very good reason;
- constantly ignoring the mutually agreed time the kids are to be picked up and returned;
- allowing a relative, a stepparent or other caregiver to take charge of the kids and their upbringing without the other parent's consent;
- contradictory rules and routines between homes;
- using a child to spy on the other parent, or having special codes and secret meetings that undermine the other parent;

- using the way your ex treats you as a reason for depriving the children of visits;
- inability to look after the children appropriately, such as neglect of their needs or lack of control;
- abuse or anger directed at the children or at each other in front of the kids;
- threats to abduct or the abduction of any of the children;
- refusing to accept that your physical or mental illness or substance abuse makes you incapable of looking after the children.

Agree to the steps you'll take if these things occur. In cases such as illness, it may mean swapping the times the kids stay with each parent. At other times such as tardiness in returning the kids, a discussion or word of warning may be sufficient. But for serious breaches such as suspected abuse, the appropriate authorities will need to be informed, which could impact on care arrangements and access to the children.

Leaving

After a break-up, most people want to put the past behind them and get on with their lives. That's easier said than done. You were one flesh, so your identity as a person is linked with your ex. Even if you're glad the relationship's over or you've begun living independent lives, it takes time to readjust habits, emotions, expectations and attitudes to living without your former spouse.

Even though planning for your exit can help you to cope, few people take time to prepare thoroughly for the parting.

Instead of a quick cut to the marriage knot, it could be less traumatic to untie it slowly through a phased withdrawal, particularly if your parting is an amicable one. It won't work when there's abuse involved, or when one of you has fallen into the arms of someone else.

With a phased withdrawal, you both agree to leave the relationship by stages. It may take weeks or months as you help each other to make the process as smooth as possible. It could also help the kids adjust to the new arrangement, and both of you to work through any issues that may arise before you finally go your separate ways.

The first stage might be for each of you to live in separate but close proximity, like different bedrooms or another apartment close by. The second stage could be to divide money and key assets, followed by the third phase of relocating to your final accommodation. The fourth phase might involve the custody arrangements for the children coming into effect, reverting to a maiden name, redirecting mail, and so on.

The final stage would be the legal divorce after a period of separation, or when either of you want to remarry. There are many ways of doing this. You need to work out what's best for your circumstances.

The advantage of the phased withdrawal is that you can come to accept being without each other and the children can adjust to their new custody arrangements. It also gives time for you both to reconsider and reverse the process if you change your minds.

The disadvantage is that it may be difficult to accept the changed conditions of your relationship while your ex is still around. It could limit your autonomy and raise issues of what is acceptable behaviour under these circumstances. Is it OK to express anger as part of your grief over the break-up? How fair is it on your ex if you want to go out with someone else or bring a date home?

Going solo

As part of your preparation for going solo, include strategies for coping with your grief and living alone.

You may have begun the grieving process well before the separation. Yet, there'll still be times when grief will hit, often when you least expect it. You might burst into tears when having coffee with a friend because it isn't with your partner, or become irrationally angry with someone who reminds you of him or her. We each react in our own way.

Men tend to grieve later and mourn the loss of their home and kids more than their ex wives. They also express their grief through actions rather than through words or emotions.

Parting is painful. Yet going through the grieving process will help you come to terms with what has happened and move on to the next phase of your life. Although the five stages of grief – denial, anger, bargaining, depression and acceptance – popularized by Elisabeth Kübler-Ross in her 1969 book, *On Death and Dying*, may apply to you, grief can take many forms and won't necessary follow a set pattern as you can have several feelings at the same time or go through a particular phase more than once.

Your grief may involve:

- shock; feelings of loss of a partner, your hopes and dreams, security, your status and maybe your control over events; feelings of numbness, emptiness, boredom, hopelessness or depression;
- feelings of betrayal, worthlessness or guilt; that you're being judged by others or are the object of their curiosity and pity;
- anger at yourself or your ex for getting married in the first place or allowing the relationship to break down;
- stress symptoms such as fatigue, sleeplessness, irritability, inability to concentrate and make decisions, disturbing dreams, lack of appetite, nausea, headaches, anxiety, difficulty coping with daily activities;
- crying, heavy drinking, smoking or drug misuse, withdrawal from others or overly depending on them for emotional support;
- denial of what went wrong or protesting over what has happened and how you're a victim;
- bargaining with your ex;
- sadness and yearning for what was good about the relationship, including idealizing your ex and the bond between you;
- acceptance of the break-up and a desire to accept responsibility and move forward.

Most former spouses find the initial loneliness hard to cope with. Diversions like watching TV dramas and movies make you feel worse because the heroes and heroines, including the divorced, always find true love and happiness. Scenes of intimacy make you nostalgic – or revolted – because they remind you of your marriage. When you go to the supermarket you'll notice other couples and happy families, which may make you lonelier.

Post-separation counselling or joining a support group, including those provided by some churches, may help you to understand what you're going through and to adjust more effectively than if you attempted to do it on your own.

Attending church, clubs and other organizations may also help you to meet others and readjust to your circumstances. You may find weekends and holidays especially hard and surround yourself with friends who support you. But because you're hurting, your friends will need to be patient and very understanding. Make a conscious decision not to unload your feelings of grief and other emotional baggage on a new date. It may make you feel better but it's unfair on the other person.

However, you may not feel ready to go on dates again for some time. Or if you do date while still grieving, you might feel you've given in to loneliness and despair.

Because the separated and divorced are more prone to illness and accidents, take steps to look after your physical health through regular balanced meals, sleep and exercise (see the section 'Your health' in Chapter 8, p. 107). Doing something physical like going for a walk, swimming or jogging might help to boost endorphins when you're feeling depressed.

Legal

Carry out what is required in any settlement agreement or court decree, like transferring vehicle ownership to one partner, changing a mortgage or other contractual debt, or dividing financial and other assets such as deposits, bonds and shares.

You may want to change your name legally back to your maiden name or to another name. If you do, you'll have to apply for a new passport, driver's licence and other identification. Don't forget to notify government agencies, voter registration, banks, credit- and charge-card agencies, loyalty programmes, insurance companies and other organizations who have you on their database.

Even if you're not changing your name, you may still need to notify organizations of your changed legal status. It might affect your rights to pension funds, tax advantages, health insurance and so on.

If you're changing address, including email address, don't wait till Christmas to let organizations and friends know. Arrange temporary redirection of mail in case you've forgotten someone.

Write a new will.

If you're going to be a solo parent with little or no income, check whether you're eligible for government assistance or help from other agencies.

Financial

Until you remove your name from joint bank accounts, credit and charge cards, you both have access to your joint funds. You could also be responsible for each other's debts. Change these as soon as possible and set up separate accounts and credit arrangements so that you're each responsible for your own funds and debts.

If you're paying alimony or child support to your ex, set these up as automatic payments so that you don't fall behind.

Make new insurance arrangements for your life, health, vehicle, home and contents.

Spiritual

Most Christian denominations uphold the sanctity of marriage. Most also accept that marriages can come unstuck (see Chapter 4, p. 36).

If you and your partner were married in a church and your denomination recognizes divorce, you may also want a church service to recognize the end of your relationship.

Your church might even have a ceremony for a couple parting but, if not, you may be able to arrange one with a celebrant. This could involve one or both of you and include a celebration of what was good in your life together, recognition that you both tried your best, a desire to learn from mistakes, and forgiveness for the hurts you've caused each other, followed by prayers for God's blessing on your separate lives in the future.

The advantage is that it's a public and spiritual declaration of your mistakes, your changed relationship and desire to move on to a new life. You're also doing this with the prayers and good wishes of those who attend. However, there will be some who will regard an end-of-marriage ceremony as a mockery of your wedding vows.

In-laws

When you married you became part of your former spouse's extended family and he or she became part of yours. Does this mean that you need to divorce yourself from each other's families?

The answer will depend on how close a friendship you have with your in-laws, what your in-laws want and what impact this will have on your ex.

> I tried to go to my family for support after we broke up but they weren't very sympathetic. They continued to see as much of my ex as me. That made me upset as I felt that she had come between me and my blood relatives.

This was how one former husband experienced his ex-wife's relationship with her in-laws. His ex-wife could have been more sensitive to his need for support, and he could have accepted more gracefully that his former wife had her own special relationship with his family. You might, of course, be delighted to leave your in-laws behind. Even so, you may need to keep in contact with them for the sake of your children.

The same could apply to your relationship with your ex-partner's friends.

Sex with your ex

Loneliness could drive you to dream of sex with your ex. You're familiar with each other and maybe the lovemaking between you was great. So why not get together occasionally to fill the arching void?

The temporary boost of getting back together could set you back emotionally by opening up the past rather than helping you to move forward. And if one of you wasn't so keen on the break-up, it may give false hopes of reconciliation. Sleeping together while you're separated could also be legal grounds to nullify an application for a divorce.

Playing fair

Try to keep any agreements you have with your spouse, including verbal promises. This will help avoid disappointment, hardship or recriminations. Let your ex – and any others who need to – know if there are problems such as not being able to provide alimony because you're between jobs. If they understand your circumstances, most people will act reasonably and find an acceptable solution.

If your partner doesn't keep an agreement, try to find out why. If there's no acceptable explanation, you may need to give a warning, followed by whatever action you've agreed to in the event of a default. As a last resort, you may have to let the courts know or take other action such as repossessing assets to pay what is due. Under such circumstances, it would be best to seek legal advice.

Accept that the relationship is over and get on with your life. Don't stalk, threaten, intimidate, pry into the life of your ex or make it difficult for him or her to have new relationships. If your ex does any of these things to you, warn him or her that such behaviour is unacceptable to you and that, if it continues, you will seek legal advice. Don't retaliate by using the same methods or threaten your ex. This is an unchristian eye-for-an-eye approach that will only make the situation worse.

If your ex persists with the undesirable behaviour, seek legal advice on whether a court order restricting what your ex can do around you is appropriate.

Respect yourself and your partner's dignity. Recognize the right for you both to have different opinions and to live separate and independent lives. Maintain a courteous and amicable climate for any ongoing dealings with your former partner.

As far as possible, try to treat your ex as a friend maybe not as a very close friend, but as a friend whom you once loved very dearly and to whom you were joined by God until the vow broke.

Further reading

―――――・◆・―――――

1 On earth as in heaven

Ambert, Anne-Marie, 'Divorce: Facts, Causes and Consequences', *Contemporary Family Trends*, rev. edn (The Vanier Institute of the Family, 2005; <http://www.vifamily.ca/library/cft/divorce>). A Canadian report which examines the factors associated with divorce, especially the causes and consequences, and argues for the importance of maintaining family values.

Born Again Christians Just as Likely to Divorce as Are Non-Christians (The Barna Group, 5 September 2004; <http://www.barna.org/barna-update/article/ 5-barna-update/194-born-again-christians-just-as-likely-to-divorce-as- are-non-christians>). US survey that found that although born-again Christians are more likely to marry than the general population, they divorce at the same rate and that most Americans do not regard divorce where adultery is not involved as a sin.

Brinig, Margaret F., and Douglas A. Allen, 'These Boots Are Made for Walking': Why Most Divorce Filers Are Women', (*American Law and Economics Review*, 2.1 [1 January 2000]), pp. 126–69. Paper suggesting that more women than men file for divorce because of their 'spouses' relative power in the marriage, their opportunities following divorce, and their anticipation of custody'.

Chan, Tak Wing, and Brendan Halpin, *The Instability of Divorce Risk Factors in the UK*, research paper (13 April 2008; <http://www.ccsr.ac.uk/esds/ events/2005-02-04/chan.pdf>). Chan from the Department of Sociology at the University of Oxford and Halpin from the Department of Sociology at the University of Limerick show how there has been a change in the divorce risk factors since the 1960s, including a lower (but still relatively high) risk for couples who cohabit and a lower risk for women who marry older and have higher educational qualifications.

'Cybersex Lures Love Cheats', BBC News (21 July 2003; <http://news.bbc. co.uk/go/pr/fr/-/2/hi/technology/3083173.stm>). Brief report of a Florida University study into infidelity via the internet, suggesting that cyber affairs are becoming more common.

Divorces in 2007 (Provisional), Selected Data Tables, England and Wales (Office for National Statistics; UK Statistics Data, 29 March 2008; <http:

158

Further reading

//www.statistics.gov.uk/statbase/Product.asp?vlnk=14124>). UK divorce information, including press release and tables on petitions filed and decrees granted; previous marital status; sex and age at divorce; couples and children of divorced couples; divorce and adoption statistics; party to whom granted and fact proven.

Harley Jr, Willard F., *His Needs, Her Needs: Building an Affair-Proof Marriage*, 15th edn (Grand Rapids, Mich.: Fleming H. Revel, 2001). Harley argues that couples must do more than just want to meet each other's needs – they must actually meet them, and gives practical advice as to how they can do that.

Montenegro, Xenia P., 'The Divorce Experience: A Study of Divorce at Midlife and Beyond' (*AARP*, May 2004; <http://research.aarp.org/general/divorce.pdf>). US survey of divorce among those over 40 years of age that found verbal, emotional or physical abuse, followed by values and lifestyle differences, were the main causes of divorce.

'Observer Sex Poll' 26 October 2008 (The *Observer*, Guardian News and Media Limited, 2009; <http://www.guardian.co.uk/lifeandstyle/2008/oct/26/observer-sex-poll-2008>). UK sex poll covering quantity and quality of sex, safe sex, education and ethnicity, home and away, manhood and monogamy.

Previti, Denise, and Paul R. Amato, 'Is Infidelity a Cause or a Consequence of Poor Marital Quality?' (*Journal of Social and Personal Relationships*, 21.2, April 2004), pp. 217–30. Research for 17 years on nearly 1,500 couples that found 'infidelity is both a cause and a consequence of relationship deterioration'.

'Relate at 70: The Country's Leading Relationships Charity Reveals the 10 Issues That Drive Couples Apart' (Relate, 8 September 2008; <http://www.relate.org.uk/PressRelease_SXC31-A77FFFD3.html>). Press report of the issues that caused couples to seek help from Relate, including affairs, dissatisfaction in the bedroom and work-life balance.

Teachman, Jay, 'Premarital Sex, Premarital Cohabitation, and the Risk of Subsequent Marital Dissolution among Women' (*Journal of Marriage & Family*, 65.2, May 2003), pp. 444–55. Results of a US study showing that women who engage in premarital sex and cohabitation have a significant risk of marriage failure but men aren't affected greatly.

'Why women regret their choice of spouse more than men' (19 August 2007; Mail Online <http://www.dailymail.co.uk/news/article-476385/Why-women-regret-choice-spouse-men.html>). Brief report of a UK survey suggesting over a fifth of women regret their choice of husband.

159

Wolcott, Ilene, and Jody Hughes, *Towards Understanding the Reasons for Divorce*, Working Paper No. 20 (Melbourne: Australian Institute of the Family, June 1999; <http://www.aifs.gov.au/institute/pubs/WP20.pdf>). Survey of divorced Australians that found emotional aspects of marriage – involving communication difficulties, incompatibility, changed lifestyle goals and infidelity – were the main reasons cited for divorce.

2 Love and marriage

Buston, Peter M., and Stephen T. Emlen, 'Cognitive Processes Underlying Human Mate Choice: The Relationship between Self-perception and Mate Preference in Western Society' (*Proceedings of the National Academy of Science*, 100.15, 2003), pp. 8805–10; <http://www.pnas.org/cgi/content/full/100/15/8805>). Survey concluding how, in Western society, we prefer partners who are similar to ourselves.

Gottman, John M., *The Seven Principles for Making a Marriage Work* (New York: Crown Publishers, 1999; <http://www.gottman.com/>). Through the use of research, case studies, questionnaires and exercises, Gottman explains how happy marriages share seven traits and unhappy couples fall short on one or more of these.

Johnston, Ian, 'Men, you have 30 Seconds to Impress Women' (*Scotsman*, 14 April 2006; <http://web.archive.org/web/20070702025413/http://news.scotsman.com/scitech.cfm?id=567952006>). Press report of research findings that women make up their minds faster than men about potential partners.

Kurdek, Lawrence A., 'The Nature and Predictors of the Trajectory of Change in Marital Quality for Husbands and Wives over the First 10 Years of Marriage' (*Journal of Developmental Psychology*, 35.5, September 1999), pp. 1283–96. Survey of over 500 Midwestern couples in the USA showing a decline in the quality of marriage over 10 years.

Kurzban, Robert, and Jason Weeden, 'HurryDate: Mate Preferences in Action' (*Evolution and Human Behavior*, 26, 2005), pp. 227–44; <ttp://www.psych.upenn.edu/PLEEP/pdfs/2005%20Kurzban%20&%20Weeden%20EHB.pdf>). Study of over 10,000 participants in HurryDate speed-dating sessions, indicating that they are driven to select partners primarily by physical attributes.

Lantin, Barbara, ' "Rules" for a Happy Marriage' (*Telegraph*, 10 May 2004; <http://www.telegraph.co.uk/health/3306958/Rules-for-a-happy-marriage.html>). Article describing research showing that happy marriages depend on negotiating a common agenda in the first few years.

Owens, Molly, 'Do Opposites Attract? Compatibility and Your Myers-Briggs Personality Type' (*Articlesbase*, 20 November 2007; <http://www.articlesbase.com/relationships-articles/do-opposites-attract-compatibility-and-your-myers-briggs-personality-type-263482.html>). Brief, easy to read article explaining Myers-Briggs Indicator personality types and partner compatibility and incompatibility.

Parker, Robyn, *Why Marriages Last: A Discussion of the Literature* (Research Paper No. 28; Melbourne: Australian Institute of Family Studies, July 2002; <http://www.aifs.org.au/institute/pubs/RP28.pdf>). A review of the research and literature of successful marriages highlighting key elements such as love, trust and respect.

Smith, Claire, 'Could this be that special someone? Best way to find out is ask a friend' (*Scotsman*, 14 February 2009; <http://thescotsman.scotsman.com/latestnews/Could-this-be-that-special.4980762.jp>). Press report of research showing friends accurately predict the outcome of a romance from the couple's body language.

Trees, Andrew, *Decoding Love: Why It Takes Twelve Frogs to Find a Prince, and Other Revelations from the Science of Attraction* (New York: Penguin, 2009). An examination of key research and theories as to how we fall in love (including smell), game theory, genetic influences on infidelity, economics and practical advice about dating.

Wallerstein, Judith S., and Sandra Blakeslee, *The Good Marriage: How and Why Love Lasts* (New York: Warner Books, 1996). Based on interviews with 50 happily married couples, the authors recognize four types of marriage – romantic, rescue, companionate and traditional – and nine tasks to undertake to make a good marriage.

Warren, Neil C., *Date . . . or Soul Mate? How to Know if Someone Is Worth Pursuing in Two Dates or Less* (Nashville, Tenn.: Thomas Nelson, 2002; <http://www.neilclarkwarren.com/index.html>). Warren stresses the importance of going beyond love chemistry and romance to find a compatible mate, by matching 29 dimensions.

3 How marriages fail

Gottman, John M., *Why Marriages Succeed or Fail: And How You Can Make Yours Last* (New York: Fireside, 1995). 'Takes you through a series of self-tests designed to help you determine what kind of marriage you have, where your strengths and weaknesses are, and what specific actions you can take to help your marriage.'

Hopper, Joseph, 'The Symbolic Origins of Conflict in Divorce' (*Journal of Marriage & Family*, 63.2, May 2001), pp. 430–45. Research describing the psychological symbols associated with conflict during the divorce process and how through mediation a cordial separation can be achieved. An earlier version of this paper is available at: <http://www.spc.uchicago.edu/prc/pdfs/hopper98-10.pdf>.

Matta, William J., *Relationship Sabotage: Unconscious Factors That Destroy Couples, Marriages, and Family* (Westport, Conn.: Greenwood, 2006). Marriage and family therapist who describes how unconscious lessons from the past can adversely affect a marriage.

'The Truth about Marriage' (*Ipsos MORI/Reader's Digest*, 18 December 2001; <http://www.ipsos-mori.com/content/the-truth-about-marriage.ashx>). Summary of a poll showing that younger men want more affection and many married people wish they weren't married.

4 Christians and divorce

Adams, Jay E., *Marriage, Divorce, and Remarriage in the Bible* (Grand Rapids, Mich.: Zondervan, 1980). A look at all the scriptural passages relating to marriage, divorce and remarriage and how these might apply to modern times.

Augustine, St, *Moral Treatises of St. Augustine* (trans. C. L. Cornish; Nicene and Post-Nicene Fathers Volume III; Christian Classics Ethereal Library; <http://www.ccel.org/ccel/schaff/npnf103.v.html>). St Augustine has had a profound influence on the Church and was the first to suggest marriage is a sacrament.

Bucer, Martin, *The Judgement of Martin Bucer Concerning Divorce* (Early Modern Literary Studies; <http://www.humanities.ualberta.ca/emls/iemls/work/etexts/mmartb.txt>). Paper presented to the English Parliament in 1644 by the poet John Milton in an attempt to sway members to take a more liberal stance on divorce.

Coxe, Cleveland (ed.), *Tertullian: Part Fourth* (Ante Nicene Fathers, Volume IV: Fathers of the Third Century; Christian Classics Ethereal Library; <http://www.ccel.org/ccel/schaff/anf04.iii.i.html>). Tertullian was a controversial Christian writer and apologist for Christianity who was against remarriage.

'Divorce in Christianity', *BBC Religion & Ethics*; <http://www.bbc.co.uk/religion/religions/christianity/ritesrituals/divorce_1.shtml>). A brief summary of divorce and remarriage in the Church of England, the Catholic Church, and other Churches.

Gorman, Michael, 'Divorce and Remarriage from Augustine to Zwingli' (*Christianity Today*, 44, August 2000 [Web-only]; <http://www.christianity-today.com/ct/2000/augustweb-only/46.0c.html>). 'How Christian understanding about marriage has changed – and stayed the same – through history.[5]

Instone-Brewer, David, *Divorce and Remarriage in the Bible: The Social and Literary Context* (Grand Rapids, Mich.: Eerdmans, 2002). Carefully researched book on the background literature and social customs of the Bible and ancient Near East, especially Judaism, providing a wide understanding of divorce and remarriage during the intertestamental period.

Instone-Brewer, David, *Divorce and Remarriage in the Church: Biblical Solutions for Pastoral Realities* (Downers Grove, Ill.: Intervarsity Press, 2003). A simplified version of his book *Divorce and Remarriage in the Bible*, with practical pastoral advice.

Instone-Brewer, David, 'What God Has Joined: What Does the Bible Really Teach about Divorce?' (*Christianity Today*, 51.10, October 2007; <http://www.christianitytoday.com/ct/2007/october/20.26.html>). Brief summary of *Divorce and Remarriage in the Bible*, maintaining grounds for divorce for Jews and the first Christians included neglect as well as adultery.

Keener, Craig S., *And Marries Another: Divorce and Remarriage in the Teaching of the New Testament* (Peabody, Mass.: Hendrickson, 1991). Explains how the early Christians would have understood the teachings of Jesus and Paul on divorce and remarriage and argues for a compassionate and forgiving attitude.

Luther, Martin, *Of Matrimony; First Principles of the Reformation or the Ninety-Five Theses and the Three Primary Works of Dr Martin Luther* (ed. Henry Wace and C. A. Buchheim; Christian Classics Ethereal Library; <http://www.ccel.org/ccel/luther/first_prin.v.iii.vi.html>). Part of this key reformer's criticisms of the Catholic Church's seven sacraments in which he argues that marriage is not a sacrament.

Marriage in Church after Divorce (updated February 2003) (The Church of England website <http://www.cofe.anglican.org/info/papers/mcad/>). Explanation of the Church of England's position on remarriage after divorce since it was approved by General Synod in 2002, with links to advice to clergy and forms for enquires.

Nobles, Sherman, *God Is a Divorcé Too! A Message of Hope, Healing and Forgiveness* (Mustang, Okla.: Tate, 2005). The title is based on Jeremiah 3.8 where God says he divorced Israel and sent her into exile for her sins. Sherman emphasizes how God continues to love and bless the divorced and their future marriages.

Origen, *Origen's Commentary on the Gospel of Matthew* (trans. John Patrick; Ante-Nicene Fathers. Volume 9: Fathers of the Third Century; Christian Classics Ethereal Library; <http://www.ccel.org/ccel/schaff/anf09.xvi.

html>). Notes on Matthew from Origen, one of the most influential of the early Christian writers.

Roberts, Alexander, and James Donaldson (eds), *Pastor of Hermes* (Ante Nicene Fathers. Volume II: Fathers of the Second Century; Christian Classics Ethereal Library; <http://www.ccel.org/ccel/schaff/anf02.ii.i.html>). Popular second-century Christian text that is included in Codex Sinaiticus, one of the oldest Christian Bibles.

The Scots Law Times (Edinburgh: W. Green & Son, 1958). In answering the question of whether artificial insemination by a donor without the husband's permission is adultery, Lord Wheatley maintains there must be genital penetration of the wife by someone who is not her husband and stated that 'a physical contact with an alien and unlawful sexual organ' is a necessary requirement for adultery.

Strauss, Mark L. (ed.), *Remarriage after Divorce in Today's Church: 3 Views* (Counterpoints: Church Life; Grand Rapids, Mich.: Zondervan, 2006). Three contributors provide different views: no marriage after divorce, remarriage on two grounds, and remarriage on a variety of grounds.

5 Justifiable breakdown

'Affairs – Satisfaction or Fatal Attraction?' (Ipsos MORI/Care for the Family, 10 February 2002; <http://www.ipsos-mori.com/content/affairs-satisfaction-or-fatal-attraction.ashx>). British survey that found a large majority of those who had an extra-marital affair found it a negative experience.

Anderson, Nancy C., *Avoiding the Greener Grass Syndrome: How to Grow Affair-Proof Hedges around Your Marriage* (Grand Rapids, Mich.: Kregal, 2004). Practical advice based on Anderson's own experiences which nearly ended her marriage, including the consequences of infidelity and ways to avoid the allure of an affair.

Fact Sheets (Relate; <http://www.relate.org.uk/mediacentre/factsheets/>). Separate fact sheets giving basic advice for couples on: arguments; communication; coping with a new baby; affairs; disruptive teenagers; empty nest syndrome; life/work balance; painful intercourse; parents separating; self-esteem; step-families; the internet and your relationship; when you've stopped having sex.

Maslow, A. H., 'A Theory of Human Motivation' (*Psychological Review*, 50, 1943, pp. 370–96; <http://psychclassics.yorku.ca/Maslow/motivation.htm>). Maslow's classic theory of motivation based on a hierarchy of needs.

Meikle, James, 'One in 25 fathers is not biological parent – study' (*Guardian*, 11 August 2005; <http://society.guardian.co.uk/children/story/0,1074,1546809,00.html>). Report of research findings at Liverpool

John Moores University that 4 per cent of fathers may not be the biological parent of a child they assume is theirs.

Waite, Linda J., Don Browning, William J. Doherty, Maggie Gallagher, Ye
Luo and Scott M. Stanley, *Does Divorce Make People Happy? Findings from
a Study of Unhappy Marriages* (Institute for American Values, 2002;
<http://www.americanvalues.org/UnhappyMarriages.pdf>). A key study
of 650 unhappily married couples in the USA that found those who
divorced where no happier than unhappy partners who stayed.

Waite, Linda J., and Maggie Gallagher, *The Case for Marriage: Why Married
People Are Happier, Healthier, and Better off Financially* (New York:
Doubleday, 2000). Research conducted by the authors showing that
committed married couples have happier and more beneficial lives than
those who are not committed to each other and that lack of commitment
and uncertainty can lead to problems and break-ups.

6 Has your marriage broken down?
See '5 Justifiable breakdown'.

7 Saving your marriage
Browne, K., 'Alleviating Spouse Relationship Difficulties' (*Counselling
Psychology Quarterly*, 8.2, 1995), pp. 109–23. Article looking at marital
relationship difficulties and the best forms of therapy or counselling for
each type, especially when spouse abuse is involved.

Doherty, William J., *Take Back Your Marriage: Sticking Together in a World
That Pulls Us Apart* (New York: Guilford Press, 2003). Examines the
popular consumer attitude to marriage and suggests ways in which
couples can connect in more permanent ways.

Jacobson, Neil S., John Gottman, *When Men Batter Women: New Insights
into Ending Abusive Relationships* (New York: Simon & Schuster, 1998).
Basing their study on research into 200 couples in dangerous relationships,
the authors suggest two types of battering style: the cobras who strike
swiftly and violently and the pit bulls who smoulder before exploding in
anger. They provide advice on how to handle both forms of violence.

Jarvis, Cheryl, *The Marriage Sabbatical: The Journey That Brings You Home*
(Cambridge, Mass.: Pegasus Publishing, 2001). Based on 55 interviews,
Jarvis's message is: 'A woman who takes time away to rejuvenate, to grow,
is in the end bringing that back to the marriage and her family.'

McKeown, Kieran et al., *Unhappy Marriages: Does Counselling Help?*
(<http://www.welfare.ie/EN/Publications/accord/Documents/acc_rpt.pdf>).
Irish report on the work of ACCORD Catholic Marriage Care Service

concluding that counselling is effective in changing a partner's behaviour and the way a partner's behaviour is perceived.

8 Stay or leave? The issues

Ahrons, Constance, *We're Still Family: What Grown Children Have to Say about Their Parents' Divorce* (New York: HarperCollins, 2004). Study of children of divorced parents interviewed over 20 years later, most of whom said that they and their parents were better off because of the divorce.

Ahrons, Constance, and Clark Champ, 'Kids and Divorce: No Lasting Damage?' (*People*, 62.2, 12 July 2004; <http://www.people.com/people/archive/article/0,,20150546,00.html>). Interview with Ahrons, who discusses her research that divorce rearranges a family but 'it does not destroy it – or the children within it'.

Booth, Alan, and Paul R. Amato, 'Parental Predivorce Relations and Offspring Postdivorce Well-being', *Journal of Marriage & Family*, 63.1, February 2001), pp. 197–212. Study that found: 'The dissolution of low-conflict marriages appears to have negative effects on offspring's lives, whereas the dissolution of high-conflict marriages appears to have beneficial effects.'

Diana, Princess of Wales, interviewed by Martin Bashir (*Panorama*, BBC current affairs programme, 24 November 1995; <http://www.bbc.co.uk/politics97/diana/panorama.html>). Transcript of the TV interview in which Princess Diana says she wants to work harder at her marriage to avoid falling into the divorce patterns of her own parents.

Hemminki, Kari, and Xinjun Li, 'Lifestyle and Cancer: Effect of Widowhood and Divorce' (*Cancer Epidemiology Biomarkers & Prevention*, 12, 2003), pp. 899–904. Swedish study showing that the loss of a spouse greatly increased the risk of all types of cancer.

Hetherington, E. Mavis, and John Kelly, *For Better or for Worse: Divorce Reconsidered* (New York: W. W. Norton, 2002. Significant study of over 1,400 families and 2,500 children over three decades that found divorce can be destructive in the short term, but can be positive in the long term.

Holmes, Thomas H., and Richard H. Rahe, 'Social Readjustment Rating Scale' (*Journal of Psychosomatic Research*, 11, 1967), pp. 213–18. Classical study based on 5,000 medical records and the way patients responded to a list of 43 stressful life events such as death or divorce that were found to affect illness.

Lucas, Richard E., Andrew E. Clark, Yannis Georgellis and Ed Diener, 'Re-examining Adaptation and the Set Point Model of Happiness:

Reactions to Changes in Marital Status' (*Journal of Personality and Social Psychology*, 84.3, 2003, pp. 527–39; <http://www.apa.org/journals/releases/ psp843527.pdf>). 'Marital transitions can be associated with long-lasting changes in satisfaction, but these changes can be overlooked when only average trends are examined.'

Raffel, Lee, *Should I Stay or Go?: How Controlled Separation (CS) Can Save Your Marriage* (Lincolnwood [Chicago], Ill.: Contemporary Books, 1999). Suggests a controlled separation that helps couples make up their minds as an alternative to couples therapy, separation or staying in an unhappy relationship.

Sun, Yongmin, and Yuanzhang Li, 'Children's Well-being during Parents' Marital Disruption Process: A Pooled Time-Series Analysis' (*Journal of Marriage & Family*, 64.2, May 2002), pp. 472–88. Study of children's academic performance and psychological well-being from three years before to three years after their parents' divorce, showing that while academic scores are affected over time, the psychological disruption increases during the divorce and decreases after the divorce.

Waite, Linda J., and Maggie Gallagher, *The Case for Marriage: Why Married People Are Happier, Healthier, and Better off Financially* (New York: Doubleday, 2000). Research conducted by the authors showing that committed married couples have happier, more beneficial lives than those who are not committed to each other, and that lack of commitment and uncertainty can lead to problems and break-ups.

Wallerstein, Judith S., Julia M. Lewis and Sandra Blakeslee, *The Unexpected Legacy of Divorce: A 25-Year Landmark Study* (New York: Hyperion, 2000). A study of 93 adults first interviewed 25 years earlier as children, concluding that children suffer the consequences of divorce long after their parents' split.

Walter, Kern, 'Should You Stay Together for the Kids?' (*Time*, 17 September 2000; <http://www.time.com/time/magazine/article/0,9171,55072,00. html>). Summary of research into the effects of divorce on children, highlighting Wallerstein and others who speak out for children of divorce.

9 Deciding your future

See '8 Stay or leave? The issues'.

10 Leaving

Ahrons, Constance, *The Good Divorce: Keeping Your Family Together When Your Marriage Comes Apart* (New York: HarperCollins, 1994). Describes and evaluates the four key types of relationship couples have with their children after a marriage break-up and gives advice to parents.

Botwinick, Amy, *Congratulations on Your Divorce: The Road to Finding Your Happily Ever After* (Deerfield Beach, Fla.: Health Communications, 2005). A women's guide to the process of divorce and how to cope with the emotional, legal and other aspects of divorce to gain a happy, healthy life.

Evans, Julie Lynn, *What about the Children? How to Help Children Survive Separation and Divorce* (London: Bantam Press, 2009). Evans maintains that children from broken homes are more distressed than parents often realize and she offers simple advice to minimize this distress and how others can help.

Fisher, Bruce, *Rebuilding: When Your Relationship Ends*, Foreword by Virginia M. Satir; 3rd edn (Atascadero, Calif.: Impact Publishers, 2005). Popular 19-step process for re-establishing yourself during and after divorce.

Kübler-Ross, Elisabeth, *On Death and Dying* (New York: Macmillan, 1969). Classic work on the grief process emphasizing the five stages: denial, anger, bargaining, depression and acceptance.

Lye, Diane N., *Scholarly Research on Post-divorce Parenting and Child Well-being*, Washington State Parenting Act Study, June 1999 (<http://www.thelizlibrary.org/liz/chap4.doc>). Review of evidence into post-divorce parenting that finds no particular advantages or disadvantages in parenting styles, but that parental conflict does have an adverse effect.

Margulies, Sam, *Getting Divorced without Ruining Your Life: A Reasoned, Practical Guide to the Legal, Emotional and Financial Ins and Outs of Negotiating a Divorce Settlement*, rev. edn (New York: Fireside, 2001). Describes the pitfalls of the adversarial system of divorce, argues for mediation during the divorce process and gives advice on how to avoid conflicts after divorce.

Wells, Rosemary, *Helping Children Cope with Divorce*, 3rd edn (London: Sheldon Press, 2003). Offers practical advice for helping children cope with the emotional and practical issues they face when parents divorce.

Index

Index

Index

phased withdrawal 110–11, 151–2
physical attraction 4, 15–16
polygamy 51
Protestant 34, 36, 37
Protestant Churches 50, 53

Rahe, Richard 108–9
realistic expectations 19–23
reconciliation 12, 31–3, 49–50, 52–3,
    63, 89, 90–1, 93, 101, 144, 156
Relationship Services 95, 137
relationships: obsessive 24; one-
    dimensional 24
respect 3, 19, 22, 24–6, 28, 34, 36,
    66–7, 70, 91, 133, 137, 157
Roman Catholic Church 3, 46–7,
    50–2
Roman Law 40
romance 5, 10, 21–2, 25, 60, 91, 105
romantic stage/phase 19, 23–4

sacrament 46–7, 50
safety: family's 72, 100, 128; personal
    62, 118, 121
Satan 43
second creation story 38
self-actualization 60
seven-year itch 4
Shammai 41
Shepherd of Hermas, The 44–5
Social Readjustment Rating Scale
    108
solo parenting 9, 106, 116, 155
soulmate 1, 97

speed date 15
splitting, high chance of 4
start-up marriages 3, 17
stepfamilies 113
stress test see Social Readjustment
    Rating Scale
successful long-lasting unions 19
Sun, Yongmin 114

Tertullian 45
Torah 37, 44
transformation stage 22
trust, between partners 5, 7, 19,
    34–5, 55, 58, 62–6, 74, 88, 93, 102,
    112, 127, 133
turning point 24–6, 28–30, 32

unbelieving spouse 1, 43, 66–7
unhappiness 9–11, 16–17, 24, 29, 33,
    35, 49, 51, 53, 58, 63, 65, 74–5, 83,
    91, 94, 100, 104–5, 107, 117, 119,
    124–7, 132, 144

Waite, Linda 75, 94–6, 104
Wallerstein, Judith 105, 113–14
Warren, Neil Clark 16–17
wedding: Christian 1–2; secular 1
wedding vows 2–3, 9, 12, 156;
    reaffirmation of 32
Wheatley, Lord 50
witness, Christian 43, 48, 54, 67,
    132–3

zero tolerance 100

171